father deficit

COL Brent V. Causey, USA (Ret)
Steven J. Gerndt, MD
Joseph A. Urcavich, DPhil

WESTBOW
PRESS
A DIVISION OF THOMAS NELSON
& ZONDERVAN

THE HOLY BIBLE, NEW INTERNATIONAL VERSION®, NIV® Copyright © 1973, 1978, 1984, 2011 by Biblica, Inc.® Used by permission. All rights reserved worldwide.

WestBow Press books may be ordered through booksellers or by contacting:

WestBow Press
A Division of Thomas Nelson & Zondervan
1663 Liberty Drive
Bloomington, IN 47403
www.westbowpress.com
1 (866) 928-1240

ISBN: 978-1-9736-2868-2 (sc)
ISBN: 978-1-9736-2867-5 (hc)
ISBN: 978-1-9736-2869-9 (e)

Print information available on the last page.

WestBow Press rev. date: 05/30/2018

CONTENTS

READER'S NOTE

MUCH OF THE CONTENT OF THIS book is the result of the combined thoughts of all three authors. There are several sections, however, that were written by one of the three authors, and this is designated at the beginning of these sections.

INTRODUCTION

MEN ARE HEAVILY INFLUENCED BY THEIR family of origin and the circumstances, whether healthy or deranged, in which they grew up. In their youth, men interpret their world through eyes of immaturity and naïveté. Their reality becomes defined by myths they create in their best effort to sort out truth. More often than not, they badly need the wisdom of a mature and emotionally developed adult male to help them find their way.

It takes a man of great courage to risk himself in the life of an adolescent in such a way that can alter the cycle. It takes a man who is willing to humble himself and earn the trust of the young boy by being honest about his imperfections and ineptitudes. For most adult men, this is unnatural and foreign. So for most young boys, that God-ordained influence is tainted or never occurs, and the cycle of anger, fear, guilt, and shame goes on.

Our desire is to disrupt that cycle by making it known there exists another way. The Genesis story gives us a glimpse of how man's journey began in relationship to God. Then man fell away and the originally perfect world was shattered. What followed was generations of repeated patterns of behavior characterized by hiding from truth and acting out of fear, shame, and guilt.

Our personal stories illustrate the manner in which these factors can play out in our own lived experience. By making an honest inward appraisal of why we respond the way we do, and by understanding what factors have heavily influenced our development, the pattern can be broken and alignment with what we were intended to become can be restored. Boys can grow into healthy, courageous, kind, devoted, and trustworthy men who seek to discover for what they were made.

(Steve:) My eldest son recently shared with me that as a young boy, he held me in high esteem. In his eyes, I was powerful, admirable, and without flaw. His perspective on his dad made me out to be someone superhuman whom no one could criticize, find fault in, or demean. My son looked at me as a man who made no mistakes and whom he could only hope to be like.

After he entered high school, although we never came to any defining conflict, there existed a distance between our hearts. I loved my son desperately, as I do all my children, yet there was a barrier to intimacy between us that neither of us acknowledged or could identify. In hindsight, he had placed me on such a pedestal that, whenever I became critical of him or tried to correct him, it became counterproductive. My thoughts about him were so important to him that if he sensed any amount of disappointment, it became demoralizing and even destructive. On the one hand, he could not accept that I might be wrong or misguided, because of how he looked at me. And on the other, for him to accept that he was less than what I expected of him was so hurtful, it put limits around his growth and development. It prevented him from fully becoming who he was, because he was so enamored with what his dad represented.

As I look back, I've come to realize I was so concerned that he succeed in life, I spent far too little time acknowledging and encouraging and loving who he already was. If I am truly honest, I was more concerned about what other people thought of him because he was my son, as opposed to being interested in helping him find out who he was meant to be. I was loving him so vigorously that I had put him in a cage. The awareness of that truth took my breath away. I can still feel the weight of this impact as I recount the past.

Ironically, it was only after my wife and I sat down with our children and shared with them the reality of our personal failures and described how their parents were flawed and imperfect, in fact sinners, that the barriers between me and my son were lifted. At first, learning about my failures, and in particular how I had let down his mom, left him reeling. Every image he had held of me was shattered; he became confused and angry. It simply did not make sense. The way he had previously defined me was now a lie.

The beautiful, amazing story about all of this is, the pain of these events led to freedom for my son, and he began to come into his own. Learning that his father was human and in fact imperfect gave him the hope he could be okay with who he was, rather than aspire to a false image of me. Most importantly, he could interact with me on a level playing field; we began to love each other as two men ought to be able to interact. We were given the opportunity to connect as father and son and man to man, without barriers and without inhibition.

I am so grateful. How much pressure my poor son must have felt. I can feel it in my breathing, a fullness in my chest. To know that he was ensnared and controlled by a lie nearly broke my heart. However, exposing the truth of the matter and coming to terms with its impact completely erased my misgivings and guilt. Instead, I can celebrate the wonderful freedom we have both encountered on the other side. I do not have to be responsible for who he becomes, and he has the freedom to make his own decisions, independent of my influence. I came to my position in life honestly, and now my son has the freedom and opportunity to do the same. It unleashed an unhappy burden for both of us, and we are better for it.

This book is written from the perspective of three men who, coming from very divergent professional and personal backgrounds, found their lives intersecting in a profound and meaningful way. Through a unique set of circumstances, their friendship and kindness toward each other has afforded them a connection, allowing them to explore the challenges of manhood and masculine development by exposing their deepest fears and most powerful hidden emotions. Through a commitment to each other characterized by honesty and vulnerability, they have uncovered and elaborated upon the behaviors and beliefs that hinder men from becoming the most freely expressed and God-honoring versions of who they were meant to be.

Divided into three parts, the book begins with a description of how the father deficit started and why men have been derailed from the onset, as it is laid out biblically in the context of Genesis. The second part illustrates this deficit through through personal stories, as told by each of the three authors. Finally, the father deficit is fully defined in Part III, where the reader is given mechanisms for understanding its impact. The road map for transcending a specific father deficit is explained.

Read on, and unravel the mystery of who you were created to be. You (or perhaps someone close to you) are a man in the making, and what you discover will be amazing.

PART I

The Father Deficit Rooted in Genesis

THE FATHER DEFICIT IS COMMON TO every human being. It began the moment Adam distanced himself from God. What began with the very first man has been perpetuated through each generation since. It is a truth we all have the opportunity to embrace and understand. Chapters 1–4 explain the biblical origin of the father deficit.

CHAPTER 1

Realistic Foundations

The apple doesn't fall far from the tree.
—German proverb

THE HUMAN STORY IS DOMINATED BY a recurring theme: the myth of independence. The basic belief behind this myth is that people can manage their own affairs without the input of others. Practically, humans accept the idea that a doctor may be useful for the body, but the needs of the soul must be handled privately, without the risk of trusting others.

This myth permeates every aspect of our culture. People who are emotionally disengaged and independent allow those closest to them to believe they can't be reached. Disengaged people signal that others don't matter and that others are not worth much to them. A father's relational ambivalence leads to children who sacrifice for others to find a sense of value. Sons will be attracted to needy women. Men who desire to be heroes will eventually be exhausted by demands they cannot meet. Daughters will seek out men who need mothering. These women will resent the distance and immaturity such men demonstrate. A woman partnered with a needy man will eventually be worn out from the stress he causes.

Given this potential impact, it would seem all of us should stop and evaluate our commitment to the myth of independence. Unfortunately, the generational pattern has been deeply ingrained

1

in human history. Commitment to the myth of independence, generation after generation, has left us unaware of the hidden forces that shape our lives.

First, I believe honesty is vital to any self-assessment. Make no mistake about it, when we are assessing our dads, objectivity is difficult to come by. Somehow, we define honesty as disrespect when talking about our families. I am not necessarily advising you to expose the gory details of your family's particular issues, but I think it's important to acknowledge the imperfections in yourself and your family.

I also think honesty requires seeking a safe, protected friendship within which to unburden your heart regarding some of the issues that make you, you. In pursuing this revelation, honesty goes from a concept to an action. You are then on the road to disrupting the patterns that have been ingrained in your life.

Next, I believe we all need mentoring in the arena of relationships. A mentor can be a friend, business acquaintance, or social associate, but it must be someone who is trustworthy and has a broader life experience than you. When you put your life on the line, you need someone to take your heart and treat it with the respect and care that comes from one who has already experienced the grace of unconditional love and acceptance.

Finally, we all need an external voice that speaks wisdom into our lives. A mentor can help you when your life reaches a decision point. This wisdom needs to be a familiar, recurring source of inspiration and insight. A mentor is a friend who is available whenever needed, who experiences your emotional break points, and who moves you toward wholeness and security.

An intellectual road map is needed to understand how your dad is wired—the historical backdrop to all masculine identities, which contributed to how you got to where you are. Once you know your history, you can acknowledge the natural weaknesses that exist in us all. In the end, we believe we all can find a renewed vision for the future by becoming a better version of who we are.

CHAPTER 2

The Common Story

THERE IS NO GREATER HIGH FOR a man than when he is engaged in something of importance and finds that his efforts have produced what he prepared for. The emotional joy of watching a work project succeed, the team you coach win, or your kids say they want to grow up to be like you has a powerful way of touching your soul. That reward is a natural prize built into each of us. You search for ways to find that internal sense of security, of knowing your life matters.

Men come by that motivation honestly. We were created to find significance in how we engage others, offer control to a world starved for direction, and clothe all our relationships with an authentic emotional intimacy. If we agree that human DNA transfers genetic characteristics from generation to generation, it follows that our relational behavior is also transferable.

In searching the Bible for answers, one method is utilizing the law of first mention. Simply put, in most cases, the first mention of a concept or purpose establishes a baseline for interpreting that concept when it reappears in situations that follow. The law of context requires that the first mention be understood in light of the new picture presented. It is through the first mention/context bifocal we will examine masculine history.

Genesis 1 gives a broad overview of the creation story. There was nothing, and from nothing, God spoke into existence something. That is an amazing, supernatural, intensely faith-driven conceptualization of life. All things from the earth to the sky—light, water, the heavens, plants, all living creatures, and ultimately humans—were spoken into existence. God's words demonstrate the power to bring into existence something from nothing.

In particular, God stated he created man in his image. Humanity was created with gender designations, but in a complementary sense to mirror the totality of God. Humans were commissioned to be like God in terms of creating life (Genesis 1:28), ruling or controlling every living thing (Genesis 1:28), nurturing and harvesting food, and providing for their own lives (Genesis 1:29). God saw what he had created and said, "This is very good" (Genesis 1:3).

There were three distinct dimensions of life that God established and reinforced in the early days of human history. God outlined human responsibility before Adam and Eve were even created. He envisioned human responsibility to be expressed through bringing order and direction to creation. Specifically, God said the concept of ruling focuses on managing through stewardship. Humanity was living in a perfect world with perfect creatures, all responding out of instinct, and we were empowered to manage these vast resources. God gave us his creatures to control, even before we existed. This was God's intention. He brought Adam and Eve into existence, and our first responsibility was to name all creatures and rule over them: control.

While we were still trying to comprehend the idea of existence, God directed us toward intimacy, the second dimension of living out his plan. Adam and Eve shared spiritual, intellectual, emotional, and physical intimacy. Procreation in its purest form was to be the norm. Intimacy, according to God's design, would result in two directed outcomes.

First, the joy and fulfillment of intimacy would lead to the creation of children. It is important to underline that when God created us, he assumed we would be involved in the act of sexual intimacy on a regular basis, with procreation leading to reproduction. Second, human sexuality and the physical connection between a man and a woman during intercourse was not an afterthought but a critical aspect of God's image. This experience between a man and a woman, with a lifelong commitment to each other, seems in itself to be an indescribable gift. But the satisfaction that comes from seeing the miracle of life come forth in one's own image, from producing a child, is unlike any other in the human experience. To know your DNA has been transferred to a new generation, to see your likeness developing in the life of a child, to live in a perfect world with perfect kids, had to produce an amazing, unfathomable sense of wonder for Adam and Eve.

Underlying both the command to control and the command to share intimacy was the expectation that humans would function with God and each other in a seamless form of engagement, the third irrevocable dimension. In a perfect world with a perfect creation, perfectly designed roles, and perfectly suited individuals to fulfill the roles, all the necessary attributes needed for engagement would be deployed. In this setting, the Godhead (Father, Son, and Spirit) walked and talked with their created couple, Adam and Eve. The Godhead demonstrated their commitment to control, engagement, and intimacy, and their created couple, Adam and Eve mirrored it. This was the pinnacle of the human historical journey, the way it was intended to be.

CHAPTER 3

Intentional Design

THE WORD *CONTROL* GETS A BAD rap in our society. People tend to recoil when it is used because they interpret it through the myth of independence. The practical result of this independent streak is that many men find it difficult to expose their weaknesses, even to their closest friends. The ironic thing is, the control we exercise through hiding creates a preoccupation in us to control others.

Did you know we were not created to control others? Our historical roots were based in honest relationships with ourselves and others. The gift of control was given to us as a responsibility by God to manage the environment he created for us. It seems the intention was for us to control processes the Creator put into place. Working and caring for the physical environment characterizes the controlling effort humans are responsible for. God put boundaries around what could be utilized and how. He also stated the obvious: he did not want man to be alone. Before resolving the issue of loneliness, God put another responsibility in the realm of control before Adam: to name all the living creatures.

So far, so good. One process after another was effectively controlled by Adam. The creation was in sync. Control was exercised the way it was intended. Adam lived the way all men dream of doing. He operated in alliance with God and was accountable to no one else.

But God saw it wasn't good for Adam to be alone. God wanted him to understand the totality of what it meant to be human in God's creation. After an exhausting day of controlling what he was assigned to control, Adam fell asleep. God removed one of Adam's ribs and made the woman out of it. Apparently there was no pain, no nightmares, nothing that would leave a lasting negative imprint. Imagine Adam's surprise when God showed up, leading this beautiful creature, Eve, to him. I am sure she was stunning and shapely and had Adam's undivided attention.

Adam's response was directed toward the Creator: "This is now bone of my bones and flesh of my flesh; she shall be called 'woman' for she was taken out of man." (Genesis 2:23). Adam named all of God's creatures, including his wife. He controlled the process; he was empowered to lead, from beginning to end. The sequence took its natural track. A new motivation in life was understood and embraced: a man was to be joined to his wife, and the two would become as one. Being joined is a recognition that life without her is not life as intended. Being joined means a natural dependence that recognizes the strengths each brings on the journey of life. Being joined cements the position that this marriage is fundamentally based in purposeful engagement. That engagement is total and unrelenting.

We know this is true because Adam and Eve were perfectly united by a perfect God in a perfect environment, and everything around them was in balance. Unimpeded engagement in that kind of environment is normal.

The final two sentences of this historical sequence tell us all we need to know: they were naked and unashamed. This is real intimacy. They personally knew who had created them. They knew what their responsibilities were and functioned in them. They shared all the benefits of the environment they inhabited. They saw the beautiful, transparent nature of each other and entered into the natural state of becoming one flesh. In this moment of intimacy, they felt no shame.

CHAPTER 4

Disruption

IN OUR WORLD, THE AMOUNT OF fraud, identity theft, and financial manipulation is staggering. Stories of greed and self-interest are unveiled daily. The funny thing is that although I may disagree with the tactics used, I cannot disregard my desire to receive the benefits of the money that was stolen. If motive for criminal action is that deeply entrenched in our being—and I believe it is—we are hopelessly ensnared unless we figure out why, own the failure personally, and reframe what drives our decisions and actions.

"Why" is not always a necessary ingredient to change, but in the case of an historical legacy, it is imperative. Generational patterns matter, and the sooner we're aware of what they are, the sooner we can disrupt them. Why would humanity risk a perfect environment, perfect relationship with their Creator, and perfect community with each other? There are three parts to the puzzle: temptation, indulgence, and disgrace.

Temptation comes to humans in many forms. This was not always true. Living in a perfect environment with perfect intimacy, fully engaged and controlling what we were asked to control, humanity had no context in which to evaluate sin. Mankind had complete moral freedom because we were created in God's image, but there was no context for sinful choices. The thought of receiving punishment or consequences for wrong decisions was simply not a relevant concept.

In this situation, the cleverest of the wild animals slithers into the picture. He speaks partial truth to the woman. It is in the form of a question to draw Eve into a false sense of control and feeling of personal value: "Did God really say, you must not eat from any tree in the garden?" (Genesis 3:1).

God had put a boundary around a particular tree (Genesis 3:3). But the problem with temptation is, it appeals to the natural inclination we have toward listening to words rather than measuring intentions. Adam and Eve had no context in which to evaluate evil, but they had the moral foundation to evaluate the outcome. They had been given specific aspects of creation to control. Obedience and submission were necessary ingredients for creation to function as created. What was now at risk was a perfect system, with perfect people, in perfect relationship, with a perfect sense of intimacy. This appears to be a simple choice over a minor issue—to take a bite of a piece of fruit—except for the hidden, overwhelming consequences.

Eve answered from a naive perspective: "You must not eat fruit from the tree in the middle of the garden, and you must not touch it, or you will die" (Genesis 3:3). I'm not sure how Eve would evaluate the potential of death. It was a foreign concept, and she had no life experience to put it into a palpable context. God had stated to Adam that the tree was not to be eaten from. Eve knew what she knew because of the engagement she had with Adam. Her response reveals who she put her faith in. It was either God or herself. This is always the choice for those of us who are people of faith. Will I trust myself or depend on God? It may not always be an either/or situation, but if it is an absolute, like "don't eat from this tree," the choice is abundantly clear.

What was the serpent's response? "'You will not certainly die,' the serpent said to the woman. 'For God knows that when you eat from it your eyes will be opened, and you will be like God, knowing good from evil'" (Genesis 3:4–5). What a dilemma. Adam and Eve are in a perfect environment, with perfect intimacy, perfect control, perfect everything, and now they are told they can become like the One who created them. Their naive, almost innocent desire is to be like God; but the promise is made intentionally by the calculated evil of Satan.

"When the woman saw that the fruit of the tree was good for food and pleasing to the eye, and also desirable for gaining wisdom, she took some and ate it. She also gave some to her husband, who was with her, and he ate it" (Genesis 3:6). Suddenly, the world of Adam and Eve changes. They realize what it means to be completely naked, emotionally exposed, with a sense of guilt hovering over their spirits and a lump of remorse sticking in their throats. They opt for the best they can do, the ultimate statement on human self-help ideas. They sew fig leaves together and make clothes for themselves. Rather than owning their miscalculated choice and action, they try to cover it up, creating yet more layers of distance from the truth and from God.

Then they hear God walking in the garden and hide from him. As if putting on clothes to cover their newly perceived nakedness were not enough, they try hiding from their sin by moving to a new location.

No such luck. Truth follows us and always inhabits our presence in one form or another. In this case, it is God himself. He asks a few questions—not because he needs an answer, but because Adam and Eve need to understand what impact their decision has made. "But the LORD God called to the man, 'Where are you?'" (Genesis 3:9). When our guard is down and we are not prepared, we don't want to hear someone pursuing us. That is a private moment; solitude is our safe place, temporarily.

Adam answers, "I heard you in the garden, and I was afraid because I was naked, so I hid" (Genesis 3:10). Once they realize nakedness is a problem, they begin to experience fear. The issue isn't Adam and Eve *being* naked; it is *realizing* they are naked.

God is relentless with Adam, as always. Once we belong to him, he diligently pursues us and solicits a response. "Who told you that you were naked? Have you eaten from the tree that I commanded you not to?" (Genesis 3:11). Shoot, being caught in the crosshairs is a discomforting position to be in.

The tension rises. Adam and Eve begin to internally break

down, and find resolution in man's favorite tactic: denial of responsibility and deflection to someone else. "The woman you put here with me gave me some fruit from the tree, and I ate it" (Genesis 3:12). Self-protection has almost no limits.

Adam attempts to distance himself by a two-step process. First, his situation is the Creator's fault. You can almost hear Adam's implied argument: "I was okay alone. You're the one who said I needed to share life with someone. If you had not forced her on me, I wouldn't be in this fix."

To which God might reply, "Listen, Adam, didn't you say, 'bone of my bone and flesh of my flesh'?"

"Okay, you're right, but she gave in to the serpent's lies. I was simply made guilty by association. What was I to do? She abandoned my leadership and made her own choice."

Engagement has moved quickly to disengagement. The emotional break between God and Adam and Eve is complete. They are still functioning in relationship, but the heart of it is a mess. Lack of trust and faith is driving distance between them all.

Adam is unaware of God's purposeful coming to him. He had been given the mantle of leadership and is held accountable by God for all that went on under his authority.

Eve mirrors what Adam has just done to her. God looks at Eve and asks, "What is this you have done?" (Genesis 3:13). Not "What was your understanding, what was your intention?" but "What have you done?"

Eve replies, "The serpent deceived me, and I ate" (Genesis 3:13). Eve blames the serpent, hoping, like Adam, to avoid any responsibility for her choice. The loss of control is coupled with disengagement and leads to the emergence of pseudo-intimacy, a false replacement for authentic interaction.

Pseudo-intimacy is usually expressed through giving another person commitment without engaging one's heart. The lack of engagement leaves those involved void of the kind of connection for which we all long. Wanting more from others becomes the longing passed on to succeeding generations. This concept distorted all aspects of the relationship between Adam and

Eve. It started with their connection to God, but moved into the marriage, parenting, and all social contexts.

It is here, at this moment in our story, the father deficit is formed. An inability to live consistently with others gives way to convenience and selfishness. From this point on, men learn to be self-centered and to struggle with submitting themselves to the needs of others, including their own spouses and children.

God responds to the human choice by acknowledging the personality that usurped his model: Satan. Evil has maintained its hold on humanity through misinformation and temptation. God curses the serpent to crawl on the earth. A state of war will exist between the serpent and Eve: "Your children will be her children's enemies. Her son will crush your head and your child will strike his heel" (Genesis 3:14–15). God then turns to the woman and says, "Your desire will be for your husband, and he will rule over you" (Genesis 3:16). A direct result of the choice that was made is the condition of conflict for control that exists in marriage (and ultimately all relationships).

God finally comes to Adam and tells him, in so many words, "You listened to your wife on an issue between you and me. Because you rejected my command, what was under your control will now be out of your control."

The last step in humanity's loss of control comes in two components. First, God chooses to cover Adam and Eve by sacrificing animals they had been commissioned to nurture (Genesis 3:21). Instead of humanity being secure in a controlled relationship, the world becomes a place where the protection of God is removed and the rules of the universe are all disrupted. Life in paradise, the garden, ends.

Man, represented through Adam, is now out of control. He is alienated from God, from his wife, Eve, and from the environment he had been commissioned to be intimately engaged with.

Total disruption. Total despair.

PART II

The Father Deficit Revealed

THE TEACHER MUST FIRST BECOME THE student to fully understand and express a concept. In this section, through personal stories of their own, the authors illustrate how the deficit has its impact in the lives and experiences of real people. They expose true disappointment and failures in order to explain how vital it is to take responsibility for the deficit through careful introspection and understanding.

Along with the personal stories, dominant themes such as guilt and anger are elaborated upon, based on what the authors realized by looking back through their histories. Although these dominant themes are not intended to be a complete reference for everyone's stories, we believe that what is presented is, at some level, common to the experience of every developing individual.

CHAPTER 5

Father Deficit 1: Steve

MY FATHER WAS A SELF-MADE MAN. I think in part because he cared for his ill mother before he reached maturity, and because he was an only child, he developed a very black-and-white understanding of right and wrong—a concrete ethos. It was not something he was taught by an adult or had modeled for him, necessarily. He acquired it through his lens on life, which showed him he had to earn his place and make choices based on what he believed was the nature of things. He was not surrounded by evil but rather by a hard-nosed, inexpressive family who taught him he had to work for what he wanted.

With his mother being progressively less independent and ultimately dying when Dad was a young man, he likely lacked much of the affirmation and affection that only a mother can give. As a consequence, the love model he was exposed to was very masculine and project-oriented. It is unlikely that any adult was vulnerable with him or verbally expressed their devotion, love, and commitment to him. All of these were implied and assumed, rather than spoken in words.

As a parent, my father was as devoted and committed to his family as any child could want. He was the consummate provider. What he did not see, or know, was how to openly and regularly express the deep love and affection he held for each of his six children. His task, as he saw it, was to equip his children with the tools to survive and succeed. In his way of seeing the world, that was fundamentally based in an ethos of honesty, knowing the difference between right and wrong, and the idea that if you worked hard enough, you could control your own destiny.

His code included always telling the truth (even if it hurts), paying your bills on time, being ten minutes early to every appointment, and competing effectively with your peers so that when opportunities became available, you were the obvious choice. It was a post-Depression belief in hard work and true grit. Affirmation came from the outcome, the victory, and the paycheck, but it rarely came from a pat on the back or an outward expression of "You are loved, and I am proud of you."

Don't misunderstand, though. He was proud of us. He was extremely pleased with his children and their accomplishments, but he did not know how to express the fact. And there is a distinct difference between admiring your children and being able to affirm them openly and regularly for the people they've become.

As a child of that environment, I was able to thrive quite well in my adolescence and early adulthood. I was academically gifted and at least capable socially. The ease with which I excelled in school made it fairly easy to succeed according to my father's definitions of life. However, I later discovered that I was lonely and had inherited the same inability to express outwardly and honestly my true emotion, especially when I felt hurt or wounded. My friends knew me as intelligent, confident, and extremely competitive. If there was ever an option, I was going to win.

My ability to work hard and meet a task head on served me well through medical school. Like many guys in my era, I deviated into alcohol and womanizing intermittently, but I was able to keep that hidden well enough that no one noticed. There must have been an angel watching over me many times. As I look back, I'm amazed that some of my poor decisions did not have greater consequences for me. But they did not. I eventually found the love of my life, who is still with me today (despite all of me), built a career as a cardiothoracic surgeon, and started a family.

Mary and I thought we had arrived. We had the career, the

house, and all that comes with financial stability. My deeply entrenched belief in excelling by diligence and hard work was proving to be true, or so I thought.

There is nothing wrong or evil about earning what you want or devoting your energies toward career success; in fact, there is something very right about these ideals. The problem arises when that is the very core of your belief system, and it's not overshadowed by a deeper commitment to loving Jesus and living for him. It becomes, as we say in medicine, pathologic. It becomes a disease.

Genesis tells us that God created Adam in his own image to be like him, and God did the same for each of us. In Matthew 10:30 and Luke 12:7, we read that "the very hairs of your head are all numbered." Going further in the verse from Luke, Jesus tells us that as we declare him Lord of our lives, he too will confess and acknowledge us before the angels of God. The most important aspect of that declaration is that God receives us not by anything we have done or accomplished, but through our faith in Jesus Christ alone.

So the very ideals and concepts by which I was raised and entered adulthood are fundamentally flawed—not because they are bad principles to live by, but because they omit the underlying truth of who we are. We are children of God, designed by him and made in his image. Each of us has been handcrafted to perfection in the eyes of our Creator. He created us, and nothing can change how he sees us; no measure of hard work or accomplishment can alter our status with God. There is nothing we can do but believe in the One who atoned, once and forever, for the devastation we were born into.

A works philosophy is easy to accept. Our human nature is to look for objective, defined, and palpable strategies to reach a goal. But a works philosophy falls short in recognizing there is no amount of accomplishment that can overcome our human nature or our predicament of being born into and inherently operating out of sin. That is for Jesus to overcome, and through our belief in him, we reach our full potential. In fact, discovering and looking toward Jesus is the only way for us to understand the true picture of who God designed us to be. It is the only way for us to pursue a life that is aligned with his purpose for us.

Every disease makes its presence known in symptoms, and symptoms usually arise at a time when our bodies are weakened by stress. In my case, the devastating illness presented not in my body, but in the body of my wife. When Mary was thirty-eight, she had a stroke, and our world was set on edge. I had relied on her for everything outside of my career. With three young children and all that goes with them, we quickly learned we were not prepared for adversity.

The stroke meant a part of her brain had died due to loss of blood flow. A small clot had entered her heart and passed into a small blood vessel in her brain, completely obstructing the delivery of red blood cells and oxygen. The result was life-threatening. Although, if you met her today, you would not recognize any deficit, the stroke was incapacitating for some time. It took her years to recover her emotional and mental well-being.

This episode fell outside of my world of understanding, and the implications it had for our marriage and family were beyond my comprehension. I responded instinctually, motivated by self-preservation, not as the servant-hearted, unconditionally loving husband I had thought I was. Emotionally, I abandoned the marriage. Soon thereafter, I fell into an affair. I was thinking only of what I thought I needed, and failing to see the bigger picture.

Together, Mary and I hit rock bottom. We became, each in our own way, truly broken.

In our brokenness, we were finally ready to receive that which we had been lacking. Adult relationships entered our lives. For me, those relationships were with men who experienced similar struggles and had come to terms with their weaknesses. Some shared similar interests but affirmed through our relationships who I was as a person, rather than what I had accomplished. My wife found friendships with women who understood her lack of identity, felt her deep pain of abandonment, and understood her need to have an unconditional commitment. They openly and honestly walked with her through a journey that led her to Christ. In this regard, my wife led, through humility and forgiveness, and I followed.

The power of a life led in devotion to the ideals of Jesus, and a marriage founded upon the triangular connection of two individuals looking vertically toward God became apparent in our lives. Piece by piece, the two of us learned what it meant to be vulnerable with each other and with God, and we opened our hearts to those around us. Previously, we had operated from a position of arrogance and pride, refusing to allow others to penetrate our inner circle. Although we did not understand it, our marriage had no true intimacy. But in embracing our brokenness and coming to terms with our imperfections and flaws as human beings, we learned to welcome others into our lives and see the fruits of vulnerable relationships that had previously been invisible.

My wife and I began to experience with eyes wide open what it meant to be members of God's church. We began pursuing alignment in all areas of our lives, including our service, the people we associated with, our social and recreational pursuits, and most importantly, the parenting of our three children.

Professionally, though, a growing issue remained in my heart. Remember, I had been raised on the fundamental idea that control of one's destiny was a matter of hard work, diligent preparation, and careful execution. For the most part, those were outstanding characteristics for a surgeon repairing the ailing hearts of his patients. But as in all things, despite the most rigorous preparation and the apparent perfection of execution, the human body is not always repairable, and sometimes patients die. The truth in medicine and surgery is, no matter how excellent the care patients receive, occasionally there's no possibility of recovery. People die. It's a fact of the human condition. Everyone eventually dies.

I functioned from the ethos upon which I was raised, which clearly stated that for one to succeed, all that was required was enough hard work. If that were true, then when I went to surgery with a living, breathing person and things went bad, that meant I must not have worked hard enough. My preparation must have been inadequate. I had failed.

This perceived failure became increasingly difficult to reconcile. As I counseled the loved ones of patients who passed away, I felt I was defending myself and operating out of guilt and shame, rather than helping them through the loss of their family member and sharing in their grief. It was an internal conflict that had no resolution.

If there was a moment in my relationship with Jesus that was most pivotal, this had to be it. While driving home one evening with that same burden (a patient had died after surgery), my emotions came to a head, and I broke down. Not knowing how to ask, I did not make any promises or offer any of my children as sacrifice. I simply said, "Lord, I can't do this anymore; please take this from me."

As if he had been waiting, the response was immediate. I did not hear any voices or see his presence, but I could feel him. What entered my mind is a message I will never forget. He simply let me know, "You are okay with me. You are enough just as you are. I made you what you are, and you have nothing to fear."

Ahhhhhhhh. I was instantly right where I needed to be. From that moment on, everything changed. For the first time in my life, I realized that I was not in control of *anything*. My role was not to determine the outcome. My role was to operate in every respect out of honesty with myself and others, and to do the most loving thing possible with the information and resources available to me at the time. The rest was up to God.

In the practice of surgery, that means I help my patients through their decision process with my expertise, and offer them my giftedness in surgery with everything I have. I can celebrate the victories with patients and their families. More importantly, I am able to participate in the grieving of the families of those who pass away—participate with love and compassion and understanding rather than guilt and shame. I know I am a better physician because of this. I can sleep in peace at night, and I have a far richer experience with my patients and their families than was remotely possible before. I hope it has made me a better husband, father, and friend as well.

One of the most compelling and meaningful relationships for me has been my friendship with Joe Urcavich, who has been and continues to be a true brother, mentor, and friend. Joe loves me because he chooses to, and he has received me with all of my baggage, without expectation. I first met Joe as a pastor, and much of what I understand about biblical truths and living as Jesus come from his teachings, but our deep connection came out of a few pointed life experiences that affected us both.

The first came on a high-altitude camping trip in Colorado that Joe led. My wife took a wrong turn on a trail, which resulted in her being lost to us for eight hours in the wilderness. Forty search and rescue personnel were commissioned, and we spent several hours imagining the worst tragedies our minds could conspire to create. Joe and I were on an emotional roller coaster with our families during that time. It ended happily when my wife was found to have deviated to a different side of the mountain, and the experience left us, as friends, much closer.

Years later, after our friendship had grown on many common levels, I received news that my father had been diagnosed with incurable cancer. On Thanksgiving Day, I went to the only person I knew would understand my pain: Joe. Together, we wept, and I was able to share my fears about what it would mean to lose my father.

Joe encouraged me to write a letter to my dad, expressing the things that Dad had never been able to express to me. Doing so opened doors in my relationship with my father and my five siblings that may have otherwise remained closed well beyond his death two years later. All thanks to Joe and his willingness to expose the pain and regrets he had learned through the loss of his own parents.

On Thanksgiving Day in 2013, six years after the death of my father, the tables were turned, and my relationship with Joe entered a new paradigm. Joe was feeling physically limited. After a barrage of testing, we discovered he had advanced coronary heart disease. He needed heart surgery, and I, one of his very good friends, was equipped to offer him the service.

Or was I? We had an open and honest conversation, together with our wives. We talked about the ethical questions involved in performing surgery on a close friend, and the potential consequences if things did not turn out well. In the end, we both arrived at the conclusion that, although it would take courage, there was no surgeon better equipped emotionally or with better expertise to meet Joe's physical needs. Together, we made the choice to walk side by side on his path to wellness.

On Thanksgiving Day, Joe received eight bypasses to his heart, and I led the team to make it happen. Joe and his wife, Arlis, spent the next three weeks after his hospital discharge recuperating at our home. This opportunity provided us a new understanding of the potential of relationships between men that otherwise could have eluded us forever. The level of trust, vulnerability, and patience we both openly embraced became the catalyst behind the writing of this book. A ministry was subsequently born, devoted to helping men understand the value and necessity of nurturing, accountable, and mentoring relationships between those of all generations, young and old.

Most profoundly, I think we came to realize that each of us is blind to certain aspects of who we are and who we were designed to become. Because we cannot see what we are blind to, it is only through the eyes of someone we trust, who loves us, and who can speak to us honestly even if it's difficult that we can realize the fullness of who we are. Men need other men in their lives.

CHAPTER 6

Redemption: Rebuilding Trust

(STEVE:) AT FACE VALUE, THE CONCEPT of rebuilding trust may be a misnomer. Once we neglect, disrupt, or abandon a relationship, it is clear that trust has been broken. The better question is, was there ever real trust in the first place? Men in particular are impatient with the journey of establishing relational ground after a relationship has been broken.

I have repeatedly heard stories from men who betrayed their wives by becoming emotionally and physically intimate with other women, and then realized that they had made poor choices. Almost always, this realization occurs only after their wives discover the problem.

For those men who turn away from the sin and truly hope to restore their marriages, there is a renewed strength in the commitment they have to their wives and families. Once they leave the affair emotionally and truly overcome their attraction to "the other woman," they are ready to participate in a healthy marriage experience again. They move relatively quickly to a state in which they are invested in their wives and are anxious for them to respond. They are willing to jump amazing hurdles to prove their devotion and loyalty.

One man in particular went so far as to take a lie detector test to prove he was not hiding anything, several years after his affair had ended. Yet he struggled to understand why his wife could not let go of the past and join him in moving forward. Men find it as easy to leave the betrayal as they did to begin it, but they have difficulty understanding why their spouses will not provide them the trust they need to move forward again in their marriages.

Quite commonly in this process, the eager husband becomes frustrated and angry with his spouse for apparently refusing to trust him. The focus of their dysfunction becomes the lack of trust rather than the episode of betrayal that began the journey. Out of his frustration, the man begins to blame the woman for their lack of intimacy, their repeated pattern of accusation and defensiveness, and their inability to love each other free of fear. This is the pattern that leads to marriages ultimately failing and dissolving, sometimes years after the event, when they had apparently survived an episode of infidelity. The man fails to find a way through to his wife because trust can never be earned, and there is no amount of doing on the part of the husband that can restore it.

Trust will only be born out of submission to the relationship on the part of the husband and the wife. Both partners must place the importance of their union (or relationship) above their own individuality. Only when each part senses unconditional grace and love overshadowing all aspects of their interactions will trust become natural and inherent. When a husband, for instance, seeks not simply to understand but to actually feel and share in the pain and hurt that is in the woman, she will know. She will sense he is seeing her for the first time, and will pour out her trust in volumes. Because she has been waiting for this since the beginning, when she experiences it, trust will be a natural response.

I find it very difficult to teach about this phenomenon, because there is clearly a supernatural component to a mutually submitted marriage that defies words and explanation. My contention, however, is that a relationship founded on real, mutual submission by definition cannot be broken. Where infidelity is concerned, trust never really existed in the first place.

Guilt becomes the operative and most influential theme in broken trust. The dynamic guilt creates in destabilizing an individual's confidence and keeping him immobilized needs to be understood. The next chapter depicts my personal observations on the topic of guilt and its power to control and destroy relationships.

CHAPTER 7

Guilt

NOTHING CAN DERAIL A PERSON FASTER, force authenticity to hide more securely, or hinder unencumbered honesty in human interactions more effectively than the presence of guilt. Guilt is an emotion that causes you to forfeit your position and yield to the emotion, the opinion, and often the control of others, because shame is the fruit of guilt. Shame tells you subconsciously that you are not worthy, you have no value, and you have no right to stand for anything.

When a felon is found guilty, the next step is punishment, a sentence to match the conviction. The individual is stripped of his clothes and dressed in a uniform. He is given a number and forced to fall in line with all the others who went before him. His identity is put aside. Guilt destroys the concept of self and imprisons that part of you that is meant to contribute—in relationship, in leadership, in friendship, and in love. When guilt has a hold on your identity and the person you are, you express a dysfunctional, defensive, bitter, and insensitive version of who you were meant to be.

When a person is discovered to have committed an offense against another, the first tendency of the guilty person is to deflect the impact of the matter, to provide excuses for the decision, and to minimize the magnitude of what has been done. The response is one of damage control, to save face from the embarrassment and humiliation. As in the case of one former president who

26

emphatically said, "I did not have sex with that woman," on national television, our first response is to defend our image, even when it is obvious there is nothing to defend. The cowardice within comes to the forefront. Instead of owning our sin, like Adam, we find it easier to deny the truth, hide, and wait like a hunted animal until the truth comes out.

Time after time, we learn that honesty is always the best policy. If we simply chose to own our bad choices, learn from them, and move on, our progress toward a better version of who we hope to be would be accelerated rather than derailed. Imagine what it would have looked like if Bill Clinton had simply said, "I behaved in a manner that was poorly representative of any man, let alone the president of the United States. I am deeply sorry for my conduct and beg forgiveness from this woman, from my wife, and from everyone impacted by my poor choices. Please accept my apology. I commit myself in the future to behavior that is requisite of the position I have accepted as the highest public official elected to serve this great country." Now, that would have been a demonstration of true leadership.

Guilt prevents a person from doing what is best or necessary in any given circumstance. When you answer to guilt, power is transferred to others, and that power has a way of controlling your behavior. It provides a wild card that can be played against you whenever needed to influence a decision, a debate, or a negotiation. Subconsciously, you fear being exposed, and dysfunction arises to cover the wound that refuses to heal. To avoid the source of guilt, you respond with reserve, anger, or even humor. You respond with deflecting behaviors that allow you to hide from the truth and avoid the risk of being recognized as imperfect, of being seen as truly human.

The end result may be different types of behavior, from bitterness to depression, but all of them result in detachment and withdrawal from your relationships. When you're ruled by guilt, you're destined to repeat a pattern of disappointment and failed interactions, which reinforces the negative image you already hold. If guilty, you begin to hate yourself, and when you hate yourself, you refuse to acknowledge affirmation or love from anyone else.

When behavior is overshadowed with guilt, it hinders authenticity and even creativity, because you are unwilling to take chances for fear of being called out or ridiculed. In a work environment, this limits your impact and contribution to the team. A lack of willingness to take a risk stifles creativity and stops the sensitive conversations required to address difficult problems and overcome unique challenges.

In personal relationships, guilt places an unspoken barrier on the honesty between you and others. There is a perception of unequal footing on your part as the guilt-ridden individual—you see yourself as less valuable or less respectable. Relational intimacy is prevented. The lack of honest expressions of love, joy, hurt, and pain leads to a disconnected and disappointing experience for both parties involved. Guilt is a staff of affliction that is used between husbands and wives, parents and children, employers and employees, and even friend and friend. Guilt is an evil tool designed, produced, and delivered by none other than Satan. It comes from the tool shop of horrors, and when used in the context of a relationship, it is the opposite of love. It is the silent destroyer of the inner spirit of an individual. Guilt, used as an action verb, is evil.

Ultimately, guilt leads to one of only two paths. It can yield bitterness and hatred, to the point where you lose all connection to anything good, such as morality, honesty, and love. You become truly evil.

Or guilt can lead you to choose love, the type of love that only God can offer. God has authored, through the birth, life, crucifixion, and resurrection of his Son, Jesus Christ, the unmatchable love that conquers all. God has declared there is nothing you have done, past, present, or future, that can separate you from him in the end. He wants you to choose love. He wants you to choose him. God tells you that you are forgiven even before you commit the sin, and he has saved a seat for you in his house. He has known you from before the world existed, and no sin can keep you from him. From God, you were whispered into being, and from Jesus, you are completely forgiven for everything. God has no interest in guilt.

When kept underground, guilt has a tendency to fester and churn and destroy like a bacterial infection that is out of control. In medicine, there is a procedure referred to as *incision and drainage*. When an infection is contained within an area of the body, it creates pressure and inflammation, leading to fevers, pain, and generalized flu-like symptoms. The bacteria eventually leaks into the bloodstream and can infect any organ in the body. The treatment is to open up the area and expose it to the air, draining the infection, relieving the pressure, and cleansing the body of the invading organism. When the abscess is drained, the immediate result is a foul, noxious odor. But it's the first step to curing the illness. Once the incision is cleaned up, the odor rapidly resolves, the patient's sense of well-being returns, and healing takes over.

Forgiveness is powerful and provides freedom, but it requires exposure. The abscess needs to be drained. Others cannot forgive what has not been openly acknowledged. There is something powerful in approaching someone you've harmed and expressing sorrow as an act of seeking forgiveness. It does not necessarily matter how that person responds, and it's never an easy task. In fact, forgiveness carries no guarantee. People can say they forgive, but have they? One never really knows. It is certainly helpful when forgiveness is offered in response to confession, but it is not required for you to move past guilt.

That is where God comes in. His requirement is that you own your sin. The important thing is that you take an honest look inward, acknowledge the error, and seek to improve. Without an honest interpretation of human nature and an awareness that you are flawed, God would be diminished. You need him because you are human, because you are imperfect, and because you are susceptible to sinful behavior.

However, for a relationship tarnished by sin to recover and flourish again, real forgiveness is a requirement. If you've been married more than a decade, you're already aware of this truth.

No human relationship can flourish without forgiveness and grace, no matter how well-intentioned those involved prove to be. Humans are flawed, and eventually everyone fails in some way, shape, or form. Think of it as the spice and flavor of relationship. Men and women wound each other, often and repeatedly. It is the nature of how we interact. In a relationship built on an unconditional commitment of love, such as marriage, the wounds have to be exposed. They have to be acknowledged honestly. Those involved need to learn from them. That is what builds strong and durable and rewarding relationships. That is what makes us better human beings. Love and grace conquer all. It's true.

CHAPTER 8

Father Deficit 2: Brent

"VISITING THE INIQUITY OF THE FATHERS on the children to the third and fourth generations" (Numbers 14:18). What does this mean? This has bothered me over and over again, to the point that, before I got married, I was sure I didn't want to have children. The question was: am I condemned already to become just like my father and continue in the folly of his sins? Not only did examining my heritage leave no room for hope, but my daily struggles with my thoughts, temper, and reactions exacerbated my fear of reacting to life just as my father did.

Many will read this opening and the similar passages in the Bible and state that I am way off in my biblical understanding of these passages. However, we know that each person will give an account of their own sins, which Ezekiel 18:19–20 makes clear:

> Yet you say, "Why should the son not bear the punishment for the father's iniquity?" When the son has practiced justice and righteousness and has observed all My statutes and done them, he shall surely live. The person who sins will die. The son will not bear the punishment for the father's iniquity, nor will the father bear the punishment for the son's iniquity; the righteousness of the righteous will be upon himself, and the wickedness of the wicked will be upon himself.

Therefore, we know that the iniquity of the fathers' sins on the children is not a simple punishment of innocent children or grandchildren for what someone else did. In these passages, the iniquity of father is passed on to the children in a different way: the children are seen as sinful and rebellious as the fathers' sin is worked out in their lives. Thus, the pattern of behaviors learned from the father is passed down from generation to generation.

There are many of examples of this repeated behavior throughout the scripture, but let us just take one. Abraham, the patriarch of the Jewish people, twice passes off Sarah, his wife, as his half sister. Although she was indeed his half sister, she was still his wife. Abraham enacts this deception after God pledges that Abraham will have prosperity and safety.

In a similar situation, Abraham's son Isaac repeats the deception and passes off his wife, Rebekah, as his sister. (Unlike Abraham and Sarah, Rebecca was not Isaac's half sister, just a cousin.) Both men's deceptions (lies) were a result of fear and lack of trust in God's promise of safety. Was this a learned behavior that Isaac received from his father? Could this be part of the iniquity passed down from the father to the child?

Understanding our family dynamics and how they influence us as men is very important to developing a healthy relationship as father and husband. In 1923 my dad was born into a home that was dysfunctional at best. His father, my grandfather, was an intelligent but uneducated man. He had only a third-grade education and turned to alcohol to cope with his inadequacies, the stresses of the Great Depression, and his inability to support his family financially. He was physically violent with both my dad and my grandmother. Dad's mother, a Choctaw Indian, was driven. She was a disciplinarian and the foundation of the family. She too did not graduate from high school.

Dad was the oldest of the three children. At age eight, he began working for the bare minimum just to help put food on the table. He delivered newspapers, collected bottles, did odd jobs, and in general did anything possible to help the finances of the family. This instilled in him a strong work ethic.

However, along with the violence that my father experienced as a child came other values that he would adopt. Some of his choices and behaviors that did not make him a stellar individual, such as stealing from and venting his temper on others, were characteristics he inherited from his father. During World War II, Dad joined the US Navy at age seventeen, and did not graduate from high school. Although Dad was always willing to work hard, his value system also allowed him to get ahead by any means available. Taking something that did not belong to him was just another way of getting a little bit ahead. He passed these values along to his children.

Although I didn't know it when I was growing up, Dad's life, values, and demeanor were not only shaped by his family but also by the effects of war. As a sailor on a battleship, he experienced the devastation of war. Many of his friends died or were permanently disabled before his eyes. He was on a landing crew that liberated Japanese prisoner of war camps and rescued the Allied prisoners. He saw the results of torture, death, and inhumanity at its worst.

After I experienced war myself as a US Army officer, and saw the effects that war has on those involved in direct combat, I realized Dad experienced severe symptoms of post-traumatic stress disorder. His disorder, of course, went unrecognized, and he certainly never received any treatment. He rarely talked about the war until I found one of his scrapbooks, which included pictures from his time rescuing POWs from prison camps. Those pictures illustrated the horrors of war.

Dad's wartime experience, combined with the physical abuse he received as a child, heavily influenced his emotional outbursts. He often had unusual reactions to common situations and seemed to go overboard. His temperament was extreme and volatile. He had unpredictable mood swings that confused me until I realized they were typical symptoms of PTSD.

Another aspect of my childhood was that my dad was never affectionate with me. At age three, I heard my parents talking about me, and they were discussing giving me up for adoption.

Talk about a blow. They didn't know that I had heard that conversation, and it was something I kept entirely to myself.

I later found out the reason for this discussion: my dad had accused my mother of cheating on him and believed that I was the product of this alleged affair. In reality, this was just another justification for his actions; he was the one who actually had an affair.

My dad was verbally abusive to my mother and both physically and verbally abusive to me. At the time, I thought this was how everyone was treated. As a result, I became a pleaser. I believed the abuse would stop and I would be rewarded with some type of affection or affirmation if I was perfect and became what others wanted me to be.

Although my paternal grandmother was somewhat religious, my dad was very antagonistic toward religion in general, Christianity in particular, and especially pastors. He expressed many times how pastors, priests, and other clergy were just out for the almighty dollar, without ever really doing a day's work. I am not sure where this attitude came from, but this thought process was expressed within our family repeatedly. If it hadn't been for my mother, I would never have been allowed to attend church. At age eight, when I asked to go to church, she said I could go as long as I was back before my dad woke up (he worked swing shift at the time), so that he would not know I had gone to church. I guess this was my form of rebellion. Since I had Mom on my side, I felt I had some security from punishment if Dad discovered I had disobeyed.

Most of the decisions I made were based on fear, obligation, or a longing for some type of recognition. My mom said that I was the perfect kid, but in reality I was just trying to avoid punishment. If I did anything that my dad perceived as wrong, he spanked me harshly.

One time I was told to be home by a certain hour, and I was five minutes late. My punishment was being spanked every half hour for a twenty-four-hour period. My dad woke me up through the night to administer the punishment.

At age nine, to cure me from biting my nails, he forced me to soak my fingers in Tabasco sauce and then put them into my mouth.

At age twelve, I truly became the perfect kid. My dad decided I was a man, and instead of using the belt, he used his fist to inflict my punishments. The first fist that connected knocked me off my feet and into the wall. Blood dripped out of my mouth. This changed my life. I learned to do whatever my dad told me. Despite my obedience, however, I still received similar punishment from time to time without any explanation of what I had done wrong.

The effects of this, the iniquities of my father, lived deep within my soul. I had battles with anger that would surface into rage. I had to isolate myself physically so I would not attack anyone. One year in elementary school, I was in fights almost every day. Of course, I always blamed others, and although I did try to avoid some of these fights, I was always pleased when the other person's action prevented me from walking away. In sixth grade, I justified beating up on two boys because they were picking on another, younger boy. This brought the fury of their parents into my home when they visited my parents. Of course, it pleased my dad that I was able to beat up two boys simultaneously. In my sophomore year of high school, the police showed up to arrest me for beating up one kid so badly, he had to have surgery on his jaw. Unfortunately (or not), no one pressed charges, so I got away with that one.

Midway through my sophomore year, I felt the call to go into full-time ministry. I knew this had to be a mistake. I had anger problems. I liked to fight. I did not have a problem with getting ahead, no matter what it took or if I needed to cheat, steal, or deceive. These, I knew, were not the attributes of a pastor or even a Christian.

I knew I had to change my life if I was going to follow this calling, but how? Becoming a Christian had not changed the deep darkness of my thoughts, although I knew right from wrong. Becoming a Christian had not changed my initial inward response to various situations, such as getting ahead no matter what.

I couldn't continue to place the responsibility for my behavior upon my dad. I prayed and prayed for these attributes to dissipate or entirely disappear. My first impulse when someone did something I didn't like was to physically lash out. How could I become a pastor? How could I have children? If they did something wrong, would I seek physical retribution against them too?

I struggled with this incongruent thought process and internal conflict. My prayers weren't working. There was no miracle for me. There was no becoming what I had been told about—a new creation. This was defeating me. I would never be good enough or enough of a man of God to be a pastor. I might not even be a Christian. Yes, I went to church, participated, led, prayed, and had my devotions, but I was failing in throwing off my old sinful nature. The sins of my father had me trapped.

When I was able to embrace God's love and forgiveness, change began to happen. This came from seeing that Paul still struggled with sin even after he became an apostle: "For I know that good itself does not dwell in me, that is, in my sinful nature. For I have the desire to do what is good, but I cannot carry it out. For I do not do the good I want to do, but the evil I do not want to do—this I keep on doing" (Romans 7:18–19).

Now do not get me wrong. I know this is not an excuse to sin freely, but it is an understanding of why I kept struggling. Struggling is normal. I do not have to give in to the struggles (sin), but they are with me in every situation. Understanding this allowed me to know that my calling into ministry was valid despite my struggles.

Therefore, at age sixteen, sometime after the last fight I ever had, I committed myself to full-time ministry. I didn't expect my dad to embrace this desire, because I knew what he though of preachers. But I didn't anticipate his reaction—that no son of his was going to become a preacher. He kicked me out of the house when I made my announcement, which threw me for a loop. Sometime later, it became clear to me that this was just what I had needed.

Being kicked out of the house because I felt the call to full-time ministry was far out of my understanding. To be honest, I think this was the first time I had cried since I overheard my parents planning to give me away at age three. To live, I camped in my car, showered at my high school, and got by with a minimum-wage job.

My favorite verse resonated in my mind amid the confusion of expulsion from my parents' home: "And we know that in all things God works for the good of those who love him, who have been called according to his purpose" (Romans 8:28). Although I did not know exactly how this verse would play out in my life, I had a burning desire to trust this promise.

CHAPTER 9

Anger: The Monster Within

(BRENT:) THERE ARE COMMON MISCONCEPTIONS IN our thinking about anger. What does anger really look like? Am I justified in my anger? Can someone else cause me to become angry? Is it ever appropriate to be angry with someone? The answers to these questions reveal how we can understand our own anger and how we employ anger in our families, with our friends, with our coworkers, and even within ourselves. This chapter will also address the appearance of anger as it expresses itself in everyday life and becomes a generational phenomenon.

For as long as I can remember, anger has been a dominant emotion in my life. Oh, I can make excuses, but in reality, no excuse is necessary. Anger exists in me. I will call it "the monster within." The way anger has been explained to me by well-meaning people, it is always wrong, and if you get angry, you are grieving the Holy Spirit. However, I have come to understand that anger is an emotion, and no matter what, everyone will experience anger.

Ephesians 4:26 states, "'In your anger do not sin': Do not let the sun go down while you are still angry." So if I read this right, "in your anger" does not mean that you won't have anger. It means "do not sin" in your anger. Anger is a normal function of who we are.

We read repeatedly that God gets angry. He was angry during

38

Noah's time, resulting in the Flood and destruction of the wicked. He was angry several times at the nation of Israel throughout the Old Testament. We know that God hates sin, and he burns with righteous anger. Righteous anger is an attribute of God, and every emotion that we have is an emotion that was given to us by God.

We likewise know that Christ experienced every emotion that we experience. In the book of Hebrews, it is said of Jesus, "For we do not have a high priest who is unable to empathize with our weaknesses, but we have one who has been tempted in every way, just as we are—yet he did not sin" (Hebrews 4:15).

I know what you are thinking: I'm just trying to justify my anger. I realize that man's anger results in nothing worthwhile. James 1:20 says that "human anger does not produce the righteousness that God desires." However, I also know, as I mentioned above, that everyone is subject to anger. Therefore, what is anger, and where does it come from?

According to Webster, anger is a "strong feeling of annoyance, displeasure, or hostility." These feelings are based on your values and beliefs, or on a significant event in your life. The anger that most of us feel is firmly rooted in our families, in the way we were raised, in the examples that we saw daily, and in the inflicted pain we were familiar with. Anger usually rears its nasty head due to a personal, internal response such as pride, arrogance, memory, or perceived injustice. That is why scripture deliberately warns against anger.

But what about righteous anger? What is this all about? We see Jesus angry at the temple when he overturns the tables of the moneychangers. We see anger between Paul and Peter as they argue over theological differences and practices. We see God's anger burn against humankind in several passages of scripture, especially against the nation of Israel for idolatry. We even see Ananias and Sapphira struck down by God because they lie to the Holy Spirit when questioned by the apostle Peter.

You might be noticing something that these examples of righteous anger have in common. Righteous anger is basically a response to things that would anger God: the wickedness of sin and its effects on humankind. Righteous anger for Christians is exhibited with pure thoughts and motives, not in seeking revenge or pronouncing judgment. Righteous anger is merely identifying the source of sin (Satan), hating that source, and praying for those who become instruments of this sin.

Scripture reminds us that vengeance is God's alone. Romans 12:19 says, "Beloved, do not avenge yourselves, but rather give place to wrath; for it is written, 'Vengeance is Mine, I will repay,' says the Lord." Although we can be defenders against injustices, this defense should be carried out without anger. We can be angry at the act of sin, but not have actionable anger in our response. We can demonstrate and proclaim with indignation that the acts of sin are wrong, but not follow up with acts of aggression. When we follow with acts of aggression, the righteousness of God is not being justifiably illustrated, and his Word is made void by our actions. Vengeance is to be left for him to claim.

This becomes confusing when Christians start talking about the death penalty, physically defending their families from personal harm, going to war, protecting their property, or fighting injustices. This chapter addresses personal anger, not the institutions of our government or its God-given authority. The authorities that exist have been established by God. Therefore, the actions of the government or of those who have the responsibility to enforce the laws fall squarely upon the governing body and not on any individual.

So what does individual anger look like? It is not righteous anger or action that is legally justified. As I mentioned before, it is the monster within. Individual anger is a response to something that we perceive as an attack, insult, emotional or physical injury, personal injustice, compromised value, or violation of beliefs. A word taken in or out of context can push that button. It can be a misunderstanding, rational or irrational. It can be pride or arrogance. It can be an attack on one's authority.

It can even be as simple as one person cutting off another in traffic. In Maryland, on a highway going into Washington, DC, there is a sign that says aggressive drivers will be prosecuted. I recently saw on the news that a driver rammed his car into another vehicle because that other driver disrespected him on the highway.

Anger comes in all shapes and sizes, and most people have no clue when it is going to erupt. A simple argument with a child about taking out the trash can blow up into an all-out war. A husband not listening to his wife while he is watching TV can become World War III. A student receiving a bad grade from a teacher can elevate what should be a civil discussion into saying hateful things, yelling, and even cursing at the teacher. All kinds of situations can result in that monster within revealing itself.

The sad truth is that anger begets anger. When we are angry, we lose all sense of compassion, grace, and forgiveness. We want revenge. It is the only thing that will feed the monster within.

The problem is that the monster has an insatiable appetite. The result of repeated encounters with anger is damage within the person who is the recipient. This damage is what we refer to as *baggage*, the sin that passes from generation to generation.

How many times have you determined that you aren't going to act inappropriately, like you remember your parents doing? I've heard this desire from many of my counseling clients. Then the confession occurs that they have become just like the people they resent and despise most—their parents. People are prone to repeat the actions they have observed, whether the action is screaming, throwing things, ignoring the issue, silence, walking out of the room, emotional attacks, verbal attacks, or physical violence. All these are actions of anger, the monster within, and they recur from generation to generation.

The key to understanding anger is to take ownership of it. Can someone really make you angry? Surprisingly, the answer is yes. If someone walked up to you and hit you, that act could made you angry. If someone threatens your family, that action would make you angry. These examples, however, are rare occurrences. Most of the time, our anger is a product of what is already within us. Unless you suffer from a psychological issue, this anger is most likely baggage that has been passed down to you from your family. While this does not justify your anger, it is one of the explanations for your anger. Since this type of behavior is generational, your parents most likely inherited it from their parents. This generational phenomenon will not stop without some person in the family making a decision to break the cycle of dysfunction.

Family of origin is not the only explanation for anger. Anger can also be born out of a critical life experience. Anger can be related to any trauma or moral injury that we encounter. It can be the result of violence that we personally experience or violent acts that we participate in. Child abuse and rape are examples of personal critical events. A soldier who's fought in direct combat or someone who has been the responsible driver in a fatal car accident are examples of participation in traumatic acts.

Participating in or observing something that goes directly against your values or belief system can result in a moral injury. Causing the death of someone, intentionally or unintentionally, may cause moral injury. Not reporting a crime or not attempting to help someone when you have the knowledge or resources may cause moral injury. Being forced to participate in or just to observe an event that you are morally opposed to can cause moral injury.

Not all people who experience a critical event or moral injury have issues with anger, but most people I have worked with express problems with managing their anger, either externally or internally. If this is you, then you have become the carrier of this disease, which potentially could pass to your children and your children's children.

So how do you break this dysfunctional problem? Earlier we read, "'In your anger do not sin': Do not let the sun go down while you are still angry, and do not give the devil a foothold" (Ephesians 4:26–27). Not giving the devil a foothold is imperative. However, this doesn't mean you will not get angry. It means that you need to manage your anger so that it doesn't result in sin. There are some Christians who think that all you need to do is pray about it and all your troubles, temptations, and problems will disappear. A relationship with God does not mean that he will take away your struggles.

Paul prayed, "I was given a thorn in my flesh, a messenger of Satan, to torment me. Three times, I pleaded with the Lord to take it away from me. But he said to me, 'My grace is sufficient for you, for my power is made perfect in weakness'" (2 Corinthians 12:7-9). This is the reality of things, especially when it has to do with an emotion that everyone is born with. It means that God will work with you, hone you, and mature you to manage each situation and temptation that you encounter. However, like everything else, that work takes time and commitment.

In our next chapter, we will look at some tools that can help you manage the monster within. I have yet to meet someone who has totally destroyed the monster, but managing the monster is a victory you can experience. The real treasure is found in how to manage anger.

CHAPTER 10

Taming the Beast

(BRENT:) FIRST OF ALL, I WANT to reiterate something I've already said. It will anger some of you and challenge others regarding your understanding of how God works. Anger, or the monster within, cannot just be prayed away.

I am not saying that if God chooses to completely neutralize a person's anger, this is impossible. I am simply saying that God acts within his creation. Since anger is an emotion, something that is attributed to God himself, it is most unlikely that God is going to act outside his creation and completely take away an emotion that can be managed, handled, and—if you'd allow me to use this term—tamed. "No temptation has overtaken you except what is common to mankind. And God is faithful; he will not let you be tempted beyond what you can bear. But when you are tempted, he will also provide a way out so that you can endure it" (1 Corinthians 10:13).

Anger is common to humankind. Everyone gets angry, but not everyone has anger issues. The temptation is in how anger expresses itself.

Some of you will argue that anger cannot be common to humankind because of Matthew 5:21-22: "You have heard that it was said to the people long ago, 'You shall not murder, and anyone who murders will be subject to judgment.' But I tell you that anyone who is angry with a brother or sister will be subject to judgment."

Just because anger is a sin does not mean that anger is not common to humankind. Look around you. Anger is so common that we see the elevation of violence everywhere merely over someone's expressed opinion. This is not just an issue for the secular world; this is something we are seeing in the Christian church. It is unreasonable to think that Christians won't get angry. Paul himself struggled with sin, and for those who have a monster within, they will struggle with it their whole lives. It's not something that goes away. However, it is something that can be managed.

So how do you go about taming this beast called anger? Foremost, there has to be a recognition that this monster dwells in you and is ready to come out anytime and anyplace. There are triggers that you know, and then there will be triggers buried deep within you that you will not know until they reveal themselves. The latter are the baggage that's been passed down from your parents, especially to men from their fathers. Triggers of anger can also come from other disruptive or traumatic critical life events, as discussed previously. The major problem for those who have the monster within is not usually a single influence, but rather cumulative life experiences. For this reason, the monster is not easily extinguished.

Recognition includes the knowledge that the monster within never produces righteous anger. Don't get me wrong; I'm not saying that people who have this monster within cannot have righteous indignation. But we know the difference. That difference is that we are masters at disguising our anger as justifiable, either by blaming someone else or saying that anyone would respond like that. A good example is "I would not have become angry over this if you had not responded to me that way." To tame the beast, you have to take personal responsibility for this anger and recognize that it exists within you.

The next step is assessing your anger. Honesty with yourself is the key. When you feel the monster within start to rear its ugly head, you have to take a step back, slowing down the anger process. This is not a new idea. The epistle of James states, "My dear brothers and sisters, take note of this: Everyone should be quick to listen, slow to speak and slow to become angry, because human anger does not produce the righteousness that God desires" (James 1:19–20). These verses are the key to effective communication, which can enhance every relationship you are in. Effective communication is essential for those who want to control their anger. You can slow your anger only when you initially feel the monster within rising up. Once the monster has risen, it is almost impossible to subdue.

Here is an example of the slowing-down process: stop, step back, and ask the question, "Why am I angry?" This is not a question to start contemplating when you are upset. This is something you should start contemplating beforehand, so you can recall it when you start to get angry. If you haven't thought about this before now, take time to consider the reasons you get angry. Take a good look at your past, your baggage, and critical events that have impacted you, and determine why you easily become angry over nonessential issues. Then take time to write your answer down so you can review it, re-evaluate it, and hone your taming skills.

Next, ask yourself, "Is my past baggage having an impact on why I am angry and how I want to respond to this anger?" What you're really asking here is whether the anger you're feeling has anything to do with the situation you're getting upset about. Most of the time, there are underlying issues that cause unreasonable or inappropriate anger. You know whether the anger you're experiencing is a normal response to the situation or is over the top. Determining the degree to which you're angry or expressing this anger can enlighten you as to whether your anger is about the current situation or if there are underlying issues that need to be dealt with.

If your anger is based on unresolved issues (baggage), then you need to assess the roots so you can respond appropriately. Assessing the roots sometimes requires illumination from an outside resource. This could be a trusted and honest friend or a mentor who is invested in a relationship with you. This could be your pastor or spiritual leader. For some issues, this might mean seeking counseling. Sometimes, taming the beast takes someone who not only will stick by you, but has permission to speak honestly and even bluntly into your life. For most people, this has to be someone outside the immediate family. Unresolved baggage is devastating to those around you. No matter your good intentions, unless you get a handle on this, you will be limited and controlled by the monster within.

You then have to address a third question: "Is this anger righteous from the other person's perspective?" I know what you are thinking—we've already addressed this. Unfortunately, when most people unleash their anger, they either feel justified at the moment or have become experts at twisting things around to justify the unharnessing of the beast. Until you come to grips with who you are in relation to your anger, you will have a tendency to look at events only from your own perspective. This results in skewed vision.

Taking the time to ask how others perceive your anger will give you a true litmus test of whether your anger is righteous or not. A good way to frame this question is, would your spouse or children be embarrassed by your anger? If the pastor were here, would he defend your actions? Would Jesus be able to stand in your defense, stating the righteousness of your anger? If so, then just maybe you have justifiable anger. The real reason for asking this question is to give ourselves time to become slow to anger.

The fourth question that is imperative to ask is, "Who am I really angry with?" Is your anger really over the situation at hand? If so, why are you taking that anger out on a person? Are you angry with yourself, with others, with the person you're currently in conflict with, or with someone who isn't even present? Until you can specify who you are angry with, you can never resolve that anger.

A lot of times, you carry your anger around with you until finally you cannot handle it any longer. Then God help the person you finally explode on. Stepping back and asking who you are really angry with allows you to focus on the actual issues and not a person who happens to be nearby. It is a key tool to taming the beast and indispensable in battling anger issues. Proverbs 29:22 notes, "An angry person stirs up conflict, and a hot-tempered person commits many sins."

Knowing the answer to these questions leads us to the next. It is a repetition of the first question: "Why am I angry?" This question gives consent to yourself to really manage or control the monster. It allows you to decide whether you want to deal with your anger or not.

Being slow to anger means more than just taking your time to get angry. There are a large number of people who take their time in getting angry, without dealing with their anger. They are the ones who usually explode improperly over insignificant issues. Being slow to anger means assessing your anger, acting righteously with your anger, and dealing with your anger in a way that is appropriate for the situation.

If you have made it this far without exploding, now come the final questions that you must ask yourself: "How do I want to deal with my anger?" and "How should I express the anger I am feeling?" Once you've given yourself permission to become slow to anger, usually by addressing the seven questions above, then you are ready to apply how God directs you to handle your anger.

Let's examine one passage that illustrates how God dealt with a rebellious people. We can apply this to ourselves as well as the nation of Israel. Exodus 34:6–7 states: "The Lord, the Lord, the compassionate and gracious God, slow to anger, abounding in love and faithfulness, maintaining love to thousands, and forgiving wickedness, rebellion and sin. Yet He does not leave the guilty unpunished; He punishes the children and their children for the sin of the parents to the third and fourth generation."

If you have the monster within, I know what you are thinking. You have skipped the first part and have gone immediately to the part where he says, "He does not leave the guilty unpunished." Again, you can justify anything with the scripture. You can say that you are just making sure that the guilty are punished. You can even claim to be an instrument of God, defending righteousness against the evil of this world.

However, before you go there, you have to apply all of scripture in context. Realize that God does not need you to dispense his punishment. He is very capable of doing this himself. Until you can rightly apply the other attributes of God listed in these verses, you do not have the upper hand to dispense God's judgment or even human anger.

First, notice that God is compassionate and gracious. He abounds in love and faithfulness, forgiving wickedness, rebellion, and sin. He is this way all the time, even when he is angry. And when he is angry, God is slow to action. Take that measuring stick out to see if you are slow to become angry.

Now we are ready to address the questions "How do you want to deal with your anger?" and "How should I express my anger?" There are two answers from scripture that I want to apply here.

> "In your anger do not sin": Do not let the sun go down while you are still angry … do not give the devil a foothold. (Ephesians 4:26–27)

> Get rid of all bitterness, rage and anger, brawling and slander, along with every form of malice. Be kind and compassionate to one another, forgiving each other, just as in Christ God forgave you. (Ephesians 4:31–32)

Notice three significant statements in these verses. The first is "In your anger do not sin." This means that you have to learn how to deal with your anger. Asking the seven questions slows you down, but to deal with the anger appropriately, you must answer the questions each and every time you get angry. Is this possible? Only if you apply prayer as you ask these questions.

The prayer that I pray is from Psalm 51:10: "Create in me a pure heart, O God, and renew a steadfast spirit within me."

Applying this prayer in these situations works for me; the beast gets tamed. You'll have to experiment with what works for you. When I don't apply this scripture passage, the monster not only raises its head, it gets loose. Destruction is the result.

Then there is the admonition "Do not give the devil a foothold." Pride, self-justification, self-righteousness, and self-reliance are ways of giving the devil a foothold. You can try to deal with your monster within by yourself, or you can get help. Help can come in many forms, but it cannot come from within yourself. You cannot deal with this alone. When one is alone, there are no checks and balances. Also, you cannot speak truth into yourself.

I know what some of you are saying: "I can do all things through Christ who strengthens me" (Philippians 4:13). Not to attack your faith, but how has that been working out for you? I tried it this way myself. I mean, was I a Christian or what? I know the scripture passage "Therefore, if anyone is in Christ, the new creation has come: The old has gone, the new is here!" (2 Corinthians 5:17). So why did I keep failing?

If it hadn't been for Paul telling of his struggles in doing what he knew he should do, I would have given up—not only on myself, but on Christianity in general. "For the good that I will to do, I do not do; but the evil I will not to do, that I practice" (Romans 7:19). Thankfully, I was invited to attend a conference that helped me see my anger issues, and I made a friend who would speak truth in my life. This was essential to being able to tame the beast.

The third significant statement from these verses is "Be kind and compassionate to one another, forgiving each other, just as in Christ God forgave you." To tame the beast, I had to apply grace with compassion. This is probably the most courageous thing I have ever done. I've been in combat numerous times, under gun and rocket fire, while serving in the army. I've played competitive sports in college and at the international level. Nothing has taken more courage and discipline than to apply grace when the monster within boils deep in my soul, wanting to explode with anger.

Grace is never deserved, so the situation doesn't have to merit the grace that is given; it is given freely. I look at myself and realize where I would be without God's grace and the many times I've received undeserved grace from those around me. This has made a huge difference for me in applying grace to others, especially when I don't feel like giving it.

There is just one more area that I must address: dealing with anger, even when you are right. Expressing justifiable anger can be very satisfying, whether it's defending an idea, a principle, a belief, a value, a cause, or a loved one. This type of justifiable, righteous anger cannot produce sin (Ephesians 4:26).

The monster within me wants to respond to anger with aggressive behavior or revenge. Aggressive behavior can be verbal or physical. Being right and being angry lose their effectiveness when you cease to manage the monster within. Holding on to that anger (letting the sun go down on your anger) or responding without kindness and compassion, even when you are right, produces sin. That sin gives way to the monster within, which results in human anger. As James 1:20 states, "Human anger does not produce the righteousness that God desires."

When you occasionally have justifiable anger, going through the seven questions will help you respond with the grace that you need. This doesn't mean that you cannot stand up for what is right, but make sure that your motives and actions are pure. When in doubt, maybe quote a verse in prayer: "Create in me a pure heart, O, God, and a steadfast spirit within me" (Psalm 51:10).

Will this always work? Can I always tame the beast? The answers to both questions are the same: no. Paul said it best:

> So I find this law at work: Although I want to do
> good, evil is right there with me. For in my inner
> being I delight in God's law; but I see another law
> at work in me, waging war against the law of my
> mind and making me a prisoner of the law of sin at
> work within me. What a wretched man I am! Who

will rescue me from this body that is subject to death? Thanks be to God, who delivers me through Jesus Christ our Lord! (Romans 7:21–25)

Although I have failures, I have found that these principles for taming the beast make me more successful when I get angry. They help me express my anger. I have fewer failures, and when I do fail, I ask for forgiveness from those I have failed and those who have observed my failure.

To continue to manage the beast within, I cannot dwell on my failures after I've asked for forgiveness. If I do, the beast within takes control. Paul gives us insight on this: "Brothers and sisters, I do not consider myself yet to have taken hold of it. But one thing I do: Forgetting what is behind and straining toward what is ahead, I press on toward the goal to win the prize for which God has called me heavenward in Christ Jesus" (Philippians 3:13–15).

We cannot strain toward what is ahead if we continue to dwell on our failures. Yes, we must learn from our mistakes and try diligently to correct them in the future. But dwelling on them will only produce more failure. Therefore, "let us throw off everything that hinders and the sin that so easily entangles. And let us run with perseverance the race marked out for us, fixing our eyes on Jesus, the author and perfecter of faith" (Hebrews 12:1–2). Then we can start taming the beast and effectively manage the monster within.

CHAPTER 11

Father Deficit 3: Joe

A FRIEND OF MINE RECENTLY SENT me a quote that said, "Failure is a learning experience, not a life sentence." That truism is easy to embrace philosophically but difficult to implement if you grew up in a religious home with perfectionist expectations. I believe the tension point in that type of home environment is based on appearances. If you look a certain way, people believe you are that way, inside and out.

What happens to the kid growing up who can play the game externally but inside is a rebellious mess? That was me. I sought and explored areas I knew were in conflict with the rules, regulations, and ethical standards expected of me. I reasoned that as long as the external facade was intact, questions would not be asked and false assumptions would be made.

I developed this dual presentation of myself to perfection. I was viewed by many around me as confident, principled, and spiritually committed. The real me was insecure, chaotic in regard to my beliefs, and confused about God's forgiveness. My choices to indulge were at his expense. My learned ability to perform for those in authority and recklessly live under the ethical radar created issues that are commonly shared issues—specifically the fear of being discovered.

I knew the deception would be fatal according to God's perspective, but my lack of character development prevented me from facing that reality. I had no courage to face this dragon.

Fear gripped my core and was continually fueled by my self-condemnation. The end result was an ongoing performance of predictably safe religious hypocrisy. In terms of how I saw this internally, it was all talk and no action.

This determination to hide from myself and to hide myself from others had direct consequences. Primary among the consequences was that I erected a false sense of grace so my self-condemning personal perspective could be normalized in a world where all were sinners. Mind you, the issue of universal sin was not the thought that was messing with me. It was my failure that had not been internally resolved. To have the answer and not be able to personally apply it is a hopeless and helpless state in which to live. Here is how it all came to be.

I was born into a lower middle-class family in the Midwest. I was fortunate to know my grandparents and relatives on both sides of the family. My mom grew up in a large Dutch immigrant family; her father had come to the country around the turn of the twentieth century. Hers was an externally strong family unit, ruled by the iron will of a quiet but direct father and a loud and controlling mother. When I look at the life choices of my mother's family, it is obvious there was a quiet rebellion that burned under the external control. My mother and her siblings loved their parents but were more intent on not disappointing them.

My dad grew up in a fragmented family. His mother's first two children were twenty years older than Dad and his brother. After my dad was born, his father abandoned his wife and two small sons. Consequently, my dad and his brother were forced to become men at about age five. They were the breadwinners, earning bits of money selling newspapers, shoveling walks in the winter, and doing any other little jobs they could find to help the three of them survive. They lived in dire poverty in the basement of a house.

When my dad talked about this part of his life, it was always with a tone of compassion for his mother. Dad learned honestly how to be a caretaker. He also learned to smooth over the immediate situation without weighing the long-term consequences. He was a smart man but had little exposure to life skills that would be taught by a father.

My parents were typical of young married couples in the 1940s and 1950s. They were separated for two years by my dad's service in the navy. Mom worked and raised my older sister, who was ten months old before my dad saw her.

During their separation, my dad's spiritual life came alive when he heard a navy chaplain share the story of Jesus. Dad had been raised in the Catholic church, embracing a form of Christianity, but prior to that story had never understood the personal nature of faith. His conversion experience left a mark on his heart that he carried throughout his life. He had been radically changed in behavior and in life direction. Like the Ancient Mariner, until the day he passed away at age eighty-six, he told his story to anyone who would listen.

After the chaos and confusion of World War II died down, my parents attempted to live the American dream: buying a house, having a family, and building a future. Dad focused on his career in sales, and Mom began to have more babies. During those early years on the journey toward their dream, Mom also had a powerful, personal encounter with God. She had been raised in the Reformed Church but had missed the difference between cultural faith and faith of the heart.

Together, my parents joined forces to raise their kids to believe that faith in Christ provided the answer to all personal ills. They spoke about their beliefs, lived their beliefs, and believed that if their children lived in a faith-based orbit, things would be perfect. Life, however, proved to be far from perfect for me and my siblings.

Like many who lived through the Great Depression and World War II, my parents were determined to make a better world. They laid aside the cultural war effort and took up the cause of changing the world for Jesus. Their patriotic focus on the war gave way to a new cause. They spent many nights away from home and their children, sharing hope with those who were down on their luck. Our modest dinner was often shared with strangers—sometimes very sketchy homeless people. For the next five decades, my parents' energy was invested in a busy rescue mission in our city. But those efforts away from home left their children unattended.

My parents often used the public platform of various churches to share their passion for changing the world through faith. Sunday evenings found me and my siblings in front of these congregations, performing and being presented as models of Christian youth. These public performances had a definite formative impact on me. As I outwardly joined my parents' worldview, which was based on almost magical qualities they assigned to faith, a dichotomy was being formed in my person. I presented publicly in a way that pleased my parents and their peers, but behind the scenes, I was experimenting in many areas. I was an imposter, and I knew it.

In retrospect, I see how my duplicity helped me compartmentalize my life. I did not even consider the emotional consequences of my choices. I acted on impulse and fulfilled my young desires, then retreated to the safety of my public image. Inside, I kept a lid on the growing sense of inconsistency, guilt, and shame that filled my heart.

This model of perfect performance versus internal, suppressed inconsistency marked my developmental years. Understand that I am analyzing my situation from a perspective of fifty years later. Over a lifetime, I've gained clarity about what these influences taught me.

My adolescent lens on values and choices continued until age nineteen, when I was kicked out of a Christian college. For the first time in my conscience life, there were internal and external consequences for my actions. Who I had been in secret was now on the table, and I could not perform my way out of that dilemma. I was a disconnected person, confused by the inconsistencies that had arisen in my life. I had been stopped by a reality that prevented me from continuing the fantasy I had crafted for those who watched me.

I now see that my external life was not integrated, to any

extent, with my internal life. The tension between the two was causing me to fragment into a plastic personality. It took years of self-reflection and much coaching and patience from mentors to connect my head with my heart. The connection process required a realization that my head knowledge (my intellect) kept me internally distant and thus unable to appraise the emotional impact of my actions. To become a whole person, I needed to feel my own emotions.

This meant moving into areas of life I didn't understand. I had to become okay with losing control over the outcome. Time and maturity provided many opportunities for me to move toward integrating my head with my heart. I look back at my early years and think about how fortunate I was to have influential people who loved me enough to risk themselves to tell me the truth. Their investment pried the lid off my pressure-loaded mind, which desperately needed relief.

Most of us spend our youth trying to distance ourselves from our fathers. In old age, we realize we have adopted their nature and outlook more than we like to admit. Our dads influence, consciously or unconsciously, every aspect of our lives. In particular, my dad shaped my skill set in relating to others.

I am sure some of us are grateful to think our dads' relational abilities have been transferred to us. Or you may think this is crazy, that you are nothing like your dad and work hard at not duplicating his limitations in your relationships.

Just as we begin to think we have compensated effectively for our fathers' deficits, we realize our surface actions may differ, but the results track along the same line. It's true in sports—when we compensate in one area, we bring pressure and sometimes injury to another. More often than not, the injury is the same: a deep bruise or torn ligament, unresolved anger or disengagement, resulting in the duplication of generational pain and injury.

"How am I doing as a father?" was the question that haunted my life until I was in my fifties. I was about eight years old, traveling with my dad on a summer work trip, when he first asked me that question. Somehow, I knew in that moment there were unstated expectations I needed to fulfill that would please the emotional need in my dad. I had no context as a child to understand his life story. As kids, most of us simply expect our parents to be grounded, secure, and able to adjust to all of life's circumstances. Little did I know that my dad, whom I love deeply, had grown up without a father.

My paternal grandmother emigrated from Austria to the United States. She had two failed marriages, gave birth to four healthy sons, and lost a daughter who died as a child. I am certain Grandma's need for emotional intimacy was realized through a relationship with my dad, who was the baby of the family. That relationship, which formed in my dad's childhood, became a major roadblock to my parents bonding deeply to each other.

When I was a child, my grandmother lived with us. According to my mom, Grandma directed the affairs of the household. My dad was blind to his emotional bond with his mom, even to the point of ignoring the constant control Grandma exerted over my mother's kitchen. Peace with his mother was more important to him than connection with his wife.

I think this dynamic was real but subconscious. I am simply acknowledging what was a part of my early life experience. I think neither of my parents were aware of the hidden patterns that caused their relational difficulties. Like most of us, they tended to blame the effects rather than look for a deeper cause. The emotional disconnect between them transferred to their children. We felt and lived the tension every day.

Fortunately, my parents had a real, committed faith. It was the singular area of life, beyond their children, that gave them a common purpose. They poured themselves into the spiritual community with abandon. When I look back it at my childhood, I wonder if my parents knew that their faith was driving the family apart. They were so busy attending Bible studies and teaching the world about Jesus that they paid little attention to the developmental process my siblings and I were experiencing.

It is vital to realize that you must understand the why behind a person's relational style to uncover generational patterns. Lack of awareness of one's own insecurities exists in every culture and is visible in most primary relationships. A common tendency is to hide and bury honest emotion when relating to others, which ultimately leads to isolation. The independent person seeks be acknowledged without risking the vulnerability that authentic relationships require. Internal conflict is directly related to the unwillingness to be seen as weak. In particular, people are very sensitive to the possibility of rejection. They may not be consciously aware of their feelings of incompetence, insecurity, and neediness. Therefore they fail to have insight into their ineffectiveness in relationships.

This is where I found myself in adolescence through early adulthood. Growing up in a faith-based home with all its expectations, spoken and unspoken, created an internal conflict that has taken me years to resolve. It centered on my desire to please my parents, which opposed my natural curiosity to explore beyond the boundaries allowed by their ideals. In retrospect, I can say with certainty that exploration without accountability leads to the isolation that accompanies hidden pain. I found that pain is rooted in conflict between the projection of one image to please my parents, while dealing with corrupt thoughts and the consequences they lead to.

As Brennan Manning says in his book, *Abba's Child*, there is an imposter in us all who is governed by fear. Manning states, "We unwittingly project onto God our own attitudes and feelings toward ourselves.... But we cannot assume He feels about us the way we feel about ourselves—unless we love ourselves compassionately, intensely, and freely." To move from negative self-judgment and guilt to the freedom of repentance, forgiveness, and self-love requires an honest look at your actions. This path also gave me insight into how I developed a duplicitous mind-set.

Authentic relationships require interdependence and an environment of safety. At the root of interdependence is an attitude fueled by a deep desire for vulnerability. Unfortunately, vulnerability—the ability to admit that others are needed to expand and enrich your life—is seen as threatening. The threat is tied to the potential loss of autonomy and the fear of being known and exposed. The thoughts behind refusing vulnerability are linked to a feeling of being controlled or manipulated.

At some point, independent people will desire to come to the end of their isolation. They will be required to take the single most important step in a process of release and freedom. They will be required to trust someone in areas beyond their control. They will be internally humbled and, consequently, externally freed to trust. That understanding of trust can blossom into a lifestyle of relational commitment, completed by the full expression of their emotions. Let me emphasize the critical nature of navigating this process with a proven, trustworthy friend.

Like most fear-based people, my journey was marked by surface relationships with many, but no deep, enriching relationships. I positioned my wife and kids at arm's length emotionally. I loved them in the same way I loved myself, which left a vacuum in both my life and theirs. I duplicated, without realizing it, what I had learned from my dad. I created a home based on external displays that were not reflected in deeply rooted values. Essentially, what others saw was not what they were really getting. My wife and children sensed this, but, like me, they did not understand the internal, systemic forces fighting inside me. The pressure built, and I felt compelled either to seek vulnerability and relational health or to stuff my confusion and manage the fallout.

I saw my wife desperate for the guy who had courted her heart. She fell for me when I conned her into believing I was intensely interested in her development, her security, and her love. In fact, I was focused on my stubbornness, my insecurity, and my self-loathing. For years, I left her isolated by my issues, my generational patterns, and my choice to not seek guidance.

My children felt the unstated rules that were communicated out of my insecurity. Unresolved issues inside of me put unspoken pressure on my kids to perform and, in a sense, forced a people-pleasing mind-set on them. Like me, they didn't want to disappoint Dad. They unconsciously were being led down the path I had followed because of my own internal chaos. I created pain for them, consciously and subconsciously, that was theirs to resolve.

I didn't do this damage intentionally. It was the natural result of growing up in a performance-driven family without internal accountability. It was rooted in the belief that if the externals looked good, we were good. My parents loved their children and created a home similar in emotional development to what they experienced. They came by their inadequacies and imperfections honestly. Once I realized that was true for me as well, the path to freedom became possible.

Freedom demanded I take on the love/hate relationship I had with pseudo-intimacy. Once I started to be grounded in who I am, I wanted to deal with my inadequacies by honestly learning about who I am, including the good, the bad, and the ugly.

CHAPTER 12

Pseudo-Intimacy

"ADAM MADE LOVE TO HIS WIFE Eve and she became pregnant and gave birth to Cain" (Genesis 4:1). Making love is different from living in a loving relationship. What had been an environment of intimacy—living in harmony with God and each other—was transferred into an environment of effort—making love. Making love is an act, not a disposition.

Adam and Eve became fully aware of the consequence of their choice. Eve recognized that God was the author of life, and he had preserved her through the pain of childbirth. The boys followed the lead of their dad, Adam. Cain worked the ground, and Abel took care of the sheep. They obviously were competing with each other for the approval of God and their dad, Adam.

When the competition came to a head, God approved of Abel's gift and rejected Cain's effort. "God said to Cain … if you do what is right will you not be accepted?" (Genesis 4:6). Without doubt, the appeal from God to do the right thing ignited in Cain a sense of disengagement from his brother that boiled over into a plan to kill him. Adam had thrown Eve under the bus, and it was understandable that his sons would pick up his example and follow suit. The unnatural act of murder was demonstrated to be a natural consequence of sin in the human experience. A brother was willing to turn disappointment into a cause to act violently toward his flesh and blood. According to the US Department of Justice, in 2009, approximately 24 percent of murder victims were killed by family members, and 53 percent were killed by someone they knew.

All this is to say the natural state of loving was destroyed in the fall. Love is no longer a disposition. What was originally designed for a world void of sin is now tainted by distrust, fear, guilt, pride, and self-preservation. The love between two brothers was replaced with jealousy and envy, and ultimately led to murder.

Human sexuality, a gift given to us by God and intended for strengthening relationship within an endorsed union between man and wife, has been infected by sin. Procreation for the purpose of populating the earth has become an afterthought in a world where human sexuality has incorporated violence in nonconsensual interactions between perpetrator and victim. Sex has been taken completely out of context. It has become a casual, selfish recreation entirely disconnected from the bond designed for marriage and for strengthening a loving, flourishing family. The authentic intimacy known by the original Adam and Eve, who were naked and unaware, was replaced by a false representation of what is possible between a man and a woman.

Out of a chaotic mess of sin and deception, *pseudo-intimacy* was born and facilitated a physical as well as spiritual disconnection from God. As God no longer walked the earth alongside mankind, pseudo-intimacy became man's best attempt at reinventing human relationship. Within it lies all of the emotions and characteristics that lead to division and compromised connection between two individuals, including insecurity, lack of trust, and competition for control. Pseudo-intimacy has become the prominent guiding foundation of every human relationship since. Now, we spend millions of dollars and countless hours of discussion and counseling trying to overcome its limitations in an effort to develop healthier, more vulnerable, and more durable interpersonal connections.

(Joe:) Time and much self-examination have revealed to me that pseudo-intimacy defined my developmental years. I remember working hard to mask the insecurity and inferiority that haunted me. I felt I could never measure up and would never be affirmed for my behavior by the adults I knew, so I looked to my peers for approval. This worked for me! They happily followed my lead and applauded my conquests and performances.

I recall having an uneasy sense that competition was my driving force at home, at school, and on the court, and it produced a growing anxiety inside me. I had to succeed, even at the expense of others. This began to complicate my relationships. The confident, cocky guy I presented was different from the insecure me. Inner conflict then began in earnest, as this behavior was against the values I had been taught at church and what I had seen my parents model.

But a nagging conscience did not deter me from continuing my well-honed way of life. Consequently, what appeared to be genuine engagement was simply a charade to find acceptance and value. This defined the dilemma of what I recognize now as pseudo-intimacy: high commitment but emotional distance. What was in it for me? What was I to do with my gregarious personality and dangerous arrogance? I intuitively knew that I was using my raw relational talent for subversive purposes, but it was my normal, and no one risked themselves to confront me with the truth of what they saw. Or perhaps some did, but I wasn't listening.

The result over time was confusion in all my close relationships. Mixed messages created chaos for those close to me. In the midst of acting out with reckless and disrespectful behavior, I was kicked out of college. It played out like this: I was called in to answer to the dean of students. Wanting to appear strong, I acted with disrespect. My bravado was challenged. I refused to back down, and I verbally abused the dean. I was asked to exit the dorm by noon that day.

In the meantime, the Vietnam War was raging and my draft number was 32. Within a few weeks, the Selective Service sent me a draft notice. My life was upended. I envisioned a two-year military tour in Southeast Asia, which meant no long-term planning. I had been determined to marry a beautiful young woman, whom I had tricked into thinking I was confident and clearheaded about the future. That draft notice was a rude reminder that I had no control over my future. I lived with a knot in my stomach and a cloud of depression over my heart.

In that emotional state, I broke my engagement to Arlis (who has since been my wife for forty-seven years). I stuffed my emotions. I felt frightened, emotionally alone, and without any desire to reach out and pursue wholeness. My fragmented soul was hung out to dry.

In the middle of this confusion, a university in the Mid-South offered me a basketball scholarship, which I quickly accepted. But it was too late. Even though I was under scholarship, my number in the draft was called. Off to Detroit I went with sixty other guys for our induction physical. Two of us ruled medically unfit for military service. One was me—I had congenital back issues. The military, my engagement to Arlis, and all things familiar were now off the table. I left for a new state and a new school.

With nothing external to lean on, I began to evaluate who I really was and envision what my life could be about. For me, this was a new idea. I experienced a enlivened sense of spirituality and purpose. I went from hiding in activity to investigating who I was. I found that I could actually love myself! Gradually, I developed an empathy for others that allowed me to examine my many failures. I owned them, repented, and sought God's forgiveness.

During this period of time, I was mentored by an amazing older man named Bob. He invested in me, teaching me specific skills for life. He modeled how to live with integrity. His belief in me gave me a new and healthy confidence.

Bob had a deep spiritual core that affected how he lived his life. Under his mentorship, I began to understand that uncovering what motivated me internally was essential to personal freedom. Those years set a new foundation in my life. I still refer to Bob's model: "It was for freedom that Christ has set us free. Stand firm" (Galatians 5:1).

A man like me who breaks from pseudo-intimacy can be free to stand firm in who he is and what he brings to those close to him. As I've traveled this path, I've embraced attitudes, behaviors, and emotions that have settled my soul and given me peace. What a relief.

PART III

The Father Deficit Healed

JOE, BRENT, AND STEVE WOULD BE the first to admit that we are on a continuous journey. There remains much to learn and more to discover about what it means to be a complete person. There is no question, however, that man was meant to pursue the fullness of life in the presence of and in partnership with other people. Living in isolation is, in fact, not living at all. We are all destined to fail in relationship over and over again, but it is the response to those failures that defines us and leads to growth. Perfection is possessed by God alone, but in his image we were created, and in honoring him, our duty is to continually chase the model he has set before us. We hope as you progress through this final section, you will begin to unravel the power and emotion of your deepest needs as an individual. The content will serve as a calling to move beyond your well-ingrained familial behaviors and traits, seeking honestly and fully to understand your limitations. By allowing others to connect with you in ways you have not previously experienced, through new levels of trust and vulnerability, you will have the opportunity to better understand yourself and how you impact the people around you. Through embracing the uniqueness of who you were designed to become, you will learn to cherish the freedom God intended.

CHAPTER 13

Mission to Maturity

THERE IS A COMMON THREAD THAT exists among people of all occupations and venues. In the military, soldiers are formed into small groups, and each member of the squad knows that protection of the other members takes precedence over everything else. There is an unspoken bond of trust and devotion that is implicit among the members of the squad, and no outside force can divide them.

Yet also among the members, disclosures of fear, pain, and suffering are kept to a minimum. Certain things are untouchable. An unwritten understanding exists that displays of vulnerability are not allowed and sensitive matters are not discussed. As a result, the emotions connected to coping with scenes of violence and loss of comrades are buried deep within their souls. Exposure of such true and very real human emotions are perceived as a lack of strength and cause others to fear that the exposed soldier will not have their backs.

In the medical community, and particularly among surgeons, there is a regular reporting of patient outcomes, results, and complications. Analysis and explanation of untoward events are conducted in a scientific and impersonal matter that resolves personal failure or mistakes in judgment. But there is no context for surgeons to discuss the emotion behind the experience of having a patient pass away as a result of an operation. While there is a visible, palpable connection between the hands of the surgeon and the patient's death, there is little acknowledgment of the internal suffering of the caregiver who attempted to save that patient's life. Typically, the culture is such that talking in depth about how it feels to lose a patient would be perceived as a weakness. Such physicians might be viewed as lacking the confidence or resilience to perform when another patient needs their technical skill. There is no acknowledgment that having a venue to safely discuss their fears of failure and loss may, in fact, be healthy and lead to improvements in future performance.

Men who are struggling relationally, especially in marriage, usually have not developed a network of other men who are dealing with similar issues. When pain sets in, men naturally resort to burying those emotions, which they are ill-equipped to handle. Suppression of their thoughts leads to larger sins like affairs, substance abuse, or gambling. Internally, men believe that others do not suffer from the same tendencies and would not understand. Rather than exposing themselves, they take the journey alone. If they have other men in their lives, those relationships exist on terms that have not established trust or allowed the kind of vulnerability that enables a man who is in pain to explore his struggles and turn away from bad decisions that could derail his personal life.

Pastors, CEOs, and other leaders, despite being surrounded by a multitude of people, usually find themselves very much alone. It is difficult to blend the need to demonstrate authority with the desire for relationship. Those in charge are put in a position where exposing how they feel could compromise their control over their congregation or team. As a result, there are very few people they can trust for counsel who would remain confidential and not thwart their ability to lead.

In the church environment, those who serve have an implicit guide for how to behave and present themselves as they carry out their duties. There is an internal conflict about whether such men participate to serve or to be served by the church. In other words, do you volunteer your service to improve your own identity, or do you volunteer purely out of a giving heart?

Parishioners put on a face they think represents the church in a favorable light. That usually means performing a role that has little connection to what they feel or who they are as people. If they said what they really thought about the people around them, they fear they might be perceived as not faithful enough.

The church model often presents a picture that members should emulate without taking into account where they started from. It results in a cookie-cutter approach to membership and eliminates the potential for individual authenticity.

The pulpit has gone to great lengths to display the positive attributes of biblical characters and has been really good at preaching what we should all strive to become. Sermon after sermon characterizes the ravages of sin and leaves the impression we should all pretend to be perfect instead of coming from a perspective that we all are flawed and fall short of God's glory. The result is a plastic environment of performers who display very little of what it means to be humble, loving, and real.

In contrast, Paul describes himself as "the worst sinner of all" (1 Timothy 1:15). Yet he became the author of most of the New Testament, God's written representation of his character and the love of Jesus. David, whom God described as a man after his own heart (1 Samuel 13:14), was a murderer and an adulterer. God loved him not as a result of David being perfect and flawless, but as a result of how David responded to his iniquities.

There are numerous other examples of work environments, family situations, social networks, and cultural contexts where the same simple tendencies play out. We have discovered that men, in particular, default to stuffing their pain and conflict. They try their best to live alone in an emotional vacuum. It is only through intentional and usually less-than-intuitive practices and behaviors that guys can move past their misconstrued beliefs about self-preservation to invite others to participate and share in their pain and suffering.

In working with men from all walks of life, our strategy has been to model vulnerability and demonstrate that we begin our interactions by exposing our personal failures. Once the shell is fractured and men see that each of us suffers from similar tendencies and weaknesses, the guard is lowered and authenticity shows up.

The irony is that people almost always function in groups and teams and congregations. Very few people stray from the group. Leaders cannot lead without people around them. Players need coaches to help them develop. Machinists need instructors to help them hone their skills. Children need parents and teachers to guide them toward behaviors that help them succeed in adulthood. People need other people to have purpose and meaning. It stands to reason that men need other men to learn what it means to become a man fully and completely.

(Steve:) One of the most remarkable people I ever encountered was a man named Fred. He and I met in college, and due to a number of connecting points, we became really good friends. He was the kind of friend who wants you to succeed. I trusted him with everything. He had a remarkably engaging spirit; when you were with Fred, he made it clear that you were the most important thing to him. He was present with the people he was around.

Fred was a playwright and musician and performer. He possessed an incredible lust for life and for people. When he was in his early twenties, he taught me how to give a gift that had real meaning. He said that I should take my favorite possession, the thing that would be hardest to part with, and give it to someone else, releasing it fully. His meaning was that to truly gift someone from your heart, the gift must be accompanied by some pain or suffering, or it would not have any real value.

Fred and I had the type of relationship that, although our lives took us in very different directions, we could come together after a period apart and begin exactly where we had left off. He became a part of my family. When my wife and I had children, Fred loved them as if they were his own. He had his own bedroom in our place. People often thought we were brothers; we even looked alike.

At age thirty-two, we moved within an hour of Fred's home and connected more frequently again. He visited us whenever he traveled because we lived near the airport he used.

At age thirty-seven, he gave me one of the greatest gifts I've ever received. He was flying to New York City to produce, off Broadway, a musical he had written, and he stopped by for a brief visit. We hiked through the woods near my home and talked. My wife and I were struggling with a number of things in our marriage, and Fred came at a good time to listen to and share in my pain. I dropped him at the airport, and as he was leaving, he paused, looked me straight in the eye, and said, "I love you."

Whaaaaaaaat? That rocked me. I was speechless and confused. I didn't know what to do with that compelling, gripping statement. I had never heard that from anyone other than my wife. And here was a man, a longtime friend, telling me what he sensed I needed—that I was important to him and he cherished my heart. I knew that it was good, but it was definitely foreign, and it took me a while to process. I felt, though, as if in that moment with Fred, I was suddenly released from something oppressive that had had its hold on me my entire life. For another man to express his love to me, in a healthy but vulnerable way, was something very new.

It would take me years to realize how powerful that moment was and, more importantly, to understand how crucial it is for masculine men to hear from others that they are loved and acknowledged. It is critical for men to know it is safe to open their hearts to other men.

For those of you who've never heard those words from your own father, I am sympathetic. It is a large void in generations of men across this planet. It is as important as the air we breathe. I am not sure how Fred figured that out, but he knew it and demonstrated it regularly with the people he was with.

Fred died a tragic and untimely death at the age of thirty-eight. There were hundreds of people at his funeral, many of whom could have referred to Fred as their best friend. How was that possible? How could one man be that significant to several hundred individuals, both female and male? Fred possessed something that many of us take years and miles to develop, and some never really come to experience. Fred accepted people for who they were and where they were in life. He risked his heart with them, expecting nothing in return. That was simply who he was.

I spent much of my life waiting for something I didn't know I needed. My overblown self-confidence and my refusal to admit I had something to learn prevented me from inviting other men into my inner circle. In order to come to terms with what we lack or to develop an awareness of where we can grow and improve as individuals, we must first open the door to self-awareness. Most men, although inwardly prideful and insecure, have to be smacked straight in the face before coming to terms with their inadequacies. Instead, they mask their insecurity by humor, sarcasm, or denial. Their confusion about intimacy and honesty in relationships is covered with anger and other controlling behaviors.

The first and most important step in overcoming the patterns we grew up under and conquering generational sin is to admit to ourselves that we may not have it all together. In order to grow and mature, a man needs to be, at some level, dissatisfied with where he is today. He must acknowledge a desire to grow and improve. He has to be willing to question and critically examine the way he has come to be, identifying the influences that have shaped his behavior.

Although some unique individuals possess this desire to improve as an inherent passion, the majority require a major life event—a financial catastrophe, a broken marriage, a health crisis, an addictive behavior—before they are truly open to mentorship and constructive criticism. Most men have to be broken, falling to rock bottom, before they can experience repair.

As I look back on specific stories in my life, when people tried to give me meaningful advice in a polite and caring way, I am 100 percent certain that their kind words fell on deaf ears. Even in conversation with my wife over years of marriage, there have been certain topics I was unwilling to listen to her perspective about. This was especially true when conversations migrated to family, my parents, or where I grew up. For some reason, whether

I agreed with her comments or not, I was not willing to allow commentary on my family, and in particular my father, unless it was positive and full of praise. Anything different would initiate a reflex. I would shut down and refuse to receive what followed.

My father set me up for success, intellectually and financially. He instilled in me a belief that I could accomplish anything I wanted. He was passionately devoted to his family. I did not want to hear anything that contradicted those successes. However, just as he was raised and admonished by men who were incomplete and imperfect, so too was I.

The second step to self-awareness is to be able to see who we are and where we came from in an objective and honest manner. Despite the power of childish fantasies and things we badly want to believe, none of us were raised by a superhero. Regardless of how great or how evil our biological father is as a figure, some things have been left out. Not a single one of us is perfect or complete. We need to look backward with clarity and honesty before we can understand what motivates us and begin the journey to becoming better.

Blind spot is defined as "a prejudice or ignorance that one has but is often unaware of." If it were written as a proverb, it would be like this: "One does not know what one cannot see." In contact sports like football and lacrosse, players learn to keep their heads on a swivel, constantly scanning for danger, because if you do not guard your blind spot, you will soon experience a "garage sale." This is an image of what a player experiences when an unexpected collision occurs and a solid hit from a defender sprays your pads, helmet, and equipment into one nasty, chaotic mess. The garage sale. If you don't uncover your blind spot, you will get hit and hit well.

After acknowledging the need to grow and accepting you have imperfections rooted in past experience, the final step in learning to develop is to actively seek the type of relationships that will provide the necessary help. Other cultures value traditions and social practices that facilitate mentorship among generations. The tribal model flourishes on behaviors that define and celebrate developmental milestones and foster productive interactions between the old and wise and the young and enthusiastic.

In many ways, the American way of life has eliminated the idea of generational mentorship. Once they enter adulthood, men typically learn to isolate, keep secret, and internalize the emotions, fears, and insecurities that are common to us all. My friendship with Fred was unique and special among young American men. It was a gift that I credit entirely to him; I would not come to recognize its true value until nearly two more decades had passed.

To be mentored and assisted in the difficult issues in life, men have to seek relationships with other men that are outside of social norms. You have to openly identify the purpose of the relationship and give permission to the other man to speak freely and without rejection about what he sees and experiences. In the same way, men have to establish a commitment to honesty with each other that is bound by a promise of safety and the desire to help each other become better. In other words, the men involved have to learn to love one another unconditionally, no matter how awkward, how painful, or how distasteful the topics they discuss might be.

Establishing such a relationship can be a challenge, and it requires a level of vulnerability that takes practice to achieve. It takes risking yourself for the sake of others, and for the sake of becoming a better man in marriage, in parenting, and in all other relationships.

The two or three others who can provide this type of meaningful connection are different for each one of us. Connection might not come in the form you expect or envision, and it often feels artificial or contrived to actively pursue such a friendship. The presence or lack of a Fred in your life is more a statement of how you present yourself and who you are than it is about the personalities around you.

Men have to learn to make themselves open to others who will speak into their lives in a meaningful way. Men are very good at outward performance and service, but have to consciously work on receiving fruitful interactions. In order to form a bond between men that facilitates maturity, at least one of the men, like Fred, has to lead and take risks. It requires you to seek the benefit of others in your life and to practice the wisdom of actually listening to the perspective of another.

Vince Lombardi is credited with many anecdotes of wisdom and experience, and he was always working toward moving people forward and encouraging them to be better. One of his most memorable motivational comments concerned driving his players to be the best but recognizing their human limitations: "Gentlemen, we will chase perfection, and we will chase it relentlessly, knowing all the while we can never attain it. But along the way, we shall catch excellence."

In this world, in order to love one another without reserve, we must recognize that we all fall short of perfection. It is important to acknowledge that each of us suffers from the same predicament. Saying with humility that there is room for improvement and that you have much to learn is the first step in opening the door to freedom in relationships with others. It is when we no longer have to be enslaved by pride and no longer have to pretend we have it all figured out that we begin to entertain the voices of others. The courage to do so can only derive from one source: to know that God is for us, and that we are forgiven.

CHAPTER 14

Where Are You Going? Fathering the Father Deficit

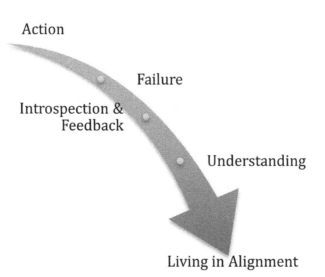

Action

Failure

Introspection & Feedback

Understanding

Living in Alignment

LIFE IS HARD. IT CALLS FOR us to continually be students—of our impact, our influence, our shortfalls, our mistakes, our own nature, our tendencies, and our opportunities for growth and improvement—so we can move toward our given purpose and design. From our parents, we receive a name, and from our family of origin, an appearance and set of genetics. But it is from God that we receive purpose and design: a reason for being here.

From the day you are born, your life is characterized by a circuitous path of behaviors, choices, and actions. Along the way, you bump into hazards, some painful, some embarrassing, and some hugely disappointing, that turn you back toward the center of the path that was previously set out for you. It seems to be a truth of human growth and development that in order to appreciate and fall in love with the straight and narrow path that was prepared for you, you must step into the sidelines, onto areas that are sharp and rugged and provide contrasting experiences.

In other words, without experiencing how bad things can truly get, you find it difficult to measure what is good. How do you recognize the temperature of perfect comfort without first knowing the pain of extreme heat or cold? Life is like that. You are like that. In order to learn who you are and what you are meant to fulfill, you need to be bumped and bruised; you need to be pushed around, to step in the mud; you need to be broken and brought to your knees. That is how you are. That is who you are.

As a man, you enter adulthood with confidence and swagger, with an attitude that you have what it takes to thrive. It works well for some, at least for a short time, but the moment inevitably comes: you lose that job you thought would take you to retirement, the promotion goes to someone else, your wife asks for a divorce, the doctor says you have an untreatable illness, you get caught drunk behind the wheel. Suddenly, what you thought was working well brings you straight to your knees. Your previous swagger finds no solution, no escape, and you are broken. Rest in that for a moment.

Something, someone is speaking to you, and you discover you are not living in alignment with who you were designed to be. You have not really understood your purpose and are not in pursuit of the very best version of who you were intended to be.

As one wise Southern preacher put it, "Be who you is, cuz if you ain't who you is, you is who you ain't."

Our culture and our stubborn nature are barriers to growth

and development. We fear correction. Criticism is received only with guilt and remorse. It becomes an assault on our character rather than an opportunity for improvement. There is a strong message of evil within us that insists we must be right and cannot be wrong. A mistake is perceived as a personal failure, as if we were perfect in every way before we even took the class on life. For some reason, we find it very difficult to admit we may have screwed up or made a bad decision or spoken out of turn. Correction is abhorrent in our common way of thinking. It takes courage to face our shortcomings directly, seek understanding, and step forward in the journey toward a better version of ourselves.

Brennan Manning said it well in his book *Ruthless Trust*:

> Our society … condemns judgment as authoritarian, dismisses acknowledgment of sin as an assault on self-worth, and resists discernment of spirits as the imposition of arbitrary standards. The devastating consequence of these shortcomings is perennial gnostic retreat from personal responsibility.
>
> If we avoid any confrontation with authentic guilt, we stifle personal growth. If we continue to blame others for our weaknesses and failures, we refuse accountability for the present direction of our life.
>
> Sin must be acknowledged and confessed before there can be forgiveness and real transformation.

God waits to respond to us until we recognize we are in need. Our way must fail before we come to our senses. We need to be broken. We have to be open to outside influence. We must become humble.

The world of heart surgery is filled with instant feedback and exhilarating experiences that are richly gratifying. There is no greater sense of accomplishment than paralyzing the heart of a human being, cutting it open to correct a defect, and watching it jump back to life once it has been put back together. To witness a still heart return to life is simply miraculous.

But—and this is where the learning comes—the heart occasionally doesn't respond as expected. Despite all good intentions, the return is less than remarkable, inadequate to sustain the patient's recovery. The personal penalty is severe for both surgeon and patient. Coping with such experience is not for the timid. Ironically, surgeons soon forget the victories, and celebration of the successes is short-lived, but the bad outcomes are seldom forgotten. It is in such instances that the character of an individual is refined and tested.

There is a saying among cardiac surgeons that "it is not the mistake but the response to the mistake that defines you." Surgeons have a duty to their patients, past, present, and future, to stare adversity in the face with courage and conviction. They must approach bad outcomes with honesty and integrity, honest about who they are and what decisions they made. They must recognize what might have contributed to an unsatisfactory result and what there is to learn for the next time. The process involves introspection, assessment of the environment, and the perspective and experience of peers and members of the operating team. Surgeons must seek the truth with the help of those around them, search for understanding, and put the new knowledge to the good work of striving to be better. The career of a surgeon should be marked by continuous growth and development. The mark of a man justified by faith in Jesus Christ is no different.

(Steve:) My wife and I have been through some incredibly tough times. As you've read, life dealt us some health and social issues we were ill prepared to handle. We both made bad choices that were based on self-protection and immaturity. We have been to some very dark and dreary places emotionally and relationally.

Yet in the end, we responded. It did not happen all at once. There were periods of decomposition amid the times of growth. However, looking back, we would not change a thing. We are immensely thankful and harbor no regret for our wounds or failures. Our joy is in the healing, and all of it is our story. Our story belongs to us and no one else. It is what brought us to where we are today: flawed and marred in every way, but simply in love with life, with each other, and with our Maker.

When Joe was released from the hospital after having a coronary artery bypass, he was tired, sore, and nauseated, and he had a limited understanding of what his recovery might look like. His physical pain and fatigue told him he was old and worn out. Despite all the promise he'd been given by the support staff, it was difficult to see the light at the end of the tunnel.

As his surgeon, I had the unique opportunity to welcome him into my home. My wife was excited about hosting Joe and his wife during his early recovery. Only a day after his release, against his instincts, I was able to coax Joe onto a treadmill for a few minutes of exercise. I proved to him he could lift a five-pound dumbbell. Without judging him or making him insecure, I walked him through a few simple exercises to demonstrate that he was still whole. I knew he was at a low point; I simply chose to lend him a hand so he could see the other side of the mountain.

As it turned out, that simple gesture proved monumental to his spirit and became a turning point in his recovery. A loving friend, not a surgeon, helped him to understand that where he had landed was temporary and where he was headed was uplifting.

Mentorship, by its very nature, has the same life-giving and spirit-enhancing characteristics. When a man with wisdom (which simply means some sort of life experience) risks himself by approaching another man out of respect, humility, and understanding, it creates a powerful momentum. Men who choose to reveal themselves to other men and then respond to their insight with acceptance and a willingness to improve always find growth and development. They become better men. They become men who are trusting and trustworthy.

Trust comes from experiencing the type of unconditional acceptance and love that Jesus demonstrated when he went to the cross. The natural and necessary response when you experience this acceptance, without being judged or criticized or made wrong, is to return it to others. The power of being accepted and loved for who you truly are is too magnificent to be stifled. It must be repeated and shared. That is how we are instructed to live.

John 13:34–35 says, "A new command I give you: Love one another. As I have loved you, so you must love one another. By this everyone will know that you are my disciples, if you love one another."

Real trust within a relationship can only occur when there is proven honesty and authenticity between the people involved. I have an old college friend, whom I will call Stan, now in his fifties, who was broken after divorcing his wife of twenty years. About a decade previously, he had gotten involved with another woman in response to the pain he was experiencing in his own marriage. He had an affair to pursue the intimacy he was lacking. After being found out, he owned his poor choice and went to many extremes over the next ten years to regain his wife's trust. He even took a lie detector test to prove to his wife he was truthful, as she had become paranoid about his every move. But the trust never returned in his marriage, and he knew that without trust, the relationship would forever be strained. Ultimately, out of frustration and the inability to regain her respect, he threw up his hands and filed for divorce. The marriage ended in sadness.

Rebuilding trust, once it is broken, can be a journey more challenging than climbing Mount Everest. Go figure. In my case, I was married to a woman who had been repeatedly let down and disappointed years before she met me. The circumstances of her childhood had taught her she had only herself to rely on when things became tough. She had developed a tremendous fear of abandonment. Our marriage was the only thing in life that she viewed as predictable and stable. I was the first and only person she never saw reason to doubt. Her relationship with me became the foundation of her strength, from which she operated as a mother, a professional, and a woman.

When I chose to be in a relationship with another woman, I

ripped away everything my wife knew as constant—everything she trusted in, everything she counted on for stability and strength. Her sense of value and significance was shattered.

It is easy to understand why it took nearly ten years for us to reestablish a durable and real trust. It is only by the power of the Holy Spirit that it was possible at all. Just like Stan, I repented earnestly from my infidelity and took many positive strides to rebuild what I had so quickly broken. Men do this from an intellectual standpoint, and we get frustrated when our spouses do not follow. My wife noticed the changes and even marveled at the transformation that was occurring within me. However, as much as she tried, and as much as she hoped, she could not regain the trust she once had in me. Every time she tested me with a jab or comment about my previous poor choices, I became defensive or angry about her lack of forgiveness and refusal to let go of the past. Like Stan, I became increasingly frustrated over our failure to resolve the impasse, and I responded, out of guilt and shame, with retaliation and anger.

At one point, I felt as though it was hopeless; our marriage was doomed. As you might imagine, my response only reaffirmed my wife's lack of trust. It reinforced her fear of abandonment, and we found ourselves in a stalemate.

Stan failed to realize the very thing that allowed me and my wife to move forward and once again thrive. I had to come to terms with my own failure. Perception of our personal sin and failure is a magnitude greater than the sin of anyone else. The ways we disappoint, hurt, or cheat others are loud, palpable, and gut-wrenching. It is painful to identify and come to terms with our personal failures. But if it were any other way, we would be entirely without a conscience.

Self-examination and internal criticism chisel away our pride, our stubbornness, and our independence from those who love us. Ultimately, we must realize that, like everyone else, we are of a sinful nature. We are products of the fall of humankind. Only one source, one power, one mediator can provide the solution to our dilemma. Jesus gave himself up on a cross to answer for all the sins that we, the human race, have committed. He provided forgiveness for everything.

My assignment was to take hold of that truth and acknowledge what had already been accomplished by submitting myself to Jesus and receiving his promise to me. I had to forgive myself for what I had done and love the man I was today, the man he created. When my wife sensed that the past no longer had a grip on me, her foundation returned. She became free, and she became beautiful. It was not her issue. It was my guilt that had been holding us back.

My wife had her own journey to take, and witnessing her develop and grow as a follower of Christ is an incredible story for another time. She was on a path parallel to mine, and we are here today as witness to the power of complete and total submission to the love of Jesus.

My struggle was rooted in my childhood. As a fifty-year-old man, I was still trying to find a sense of acceptance and acknowledgment. I had not received it from my dad, I could not find it in my occupation, and now I was learning I would not find my identity in my marriage.

This is where men like Fred and other special heroes have made an incredible difference in my life. I chose to confide in and listen to these men, who were vulnerable with me and allowed me to be real with them. They taught me about the love of God. He alone possesses the power of true forgiveness. He is the one and only source of my true identity. Complete and utter submission to the One who created me, the One who knows my every move, my every emotion, and my every thought, was the only way I could become comfortable as the man I was created to be. I know that I have a purpose, and although I will continue to stumble and fall, I know the source of my strength is in he who made me, not in the things or people of this world. I suspect he laughed uncontrollably, watching it all unfold. I must have been an enormous source of entertainment. (You are welcome, God.)

When I became confident in what defined me as a man and was honest with myself about who I was today, I no longer felt guilt and shame from the learnings of the past. The subconscious behavior and emotion and body language that my wife was now witnessing expressed an entirely different paradigm. The defensiveness and retaliation she was used to had vanished. I had become tender to the tragedy of what she had lost and how deeply she longed for the intimacy with me that had not yet been regained. I began to love her for who she was and where she was, and my spite and venom waned. When I began to appreciate what she needed and stopped reacting negatively to her emotions, things changed.

Because I was solid in my intentions and operated out of belief in my meaning and purpose, the message I was sending, subliminal as well as overt, told my wife that I was strong and powerful, that I was reliable, and that my love for her was unconditional. That is how Jesus loves me, and as a result, that is how I am able to love my wife.

Forgiveness is powerful, and we are testimony to this truth. Reconciliation and redemption are possible and active in this world. Thank God for the real, courageous men I have come to know and who know me.

Living in Alignment

The sure symptoms of a life led by uncertainty and without direction are anger and anxiety and pressured emotion that looks out of proportion to reality. In contrast, the presence of a man who embraces what he was designed for and who understands his purpose is characterized by peace, consistency, and humility, even in times of crisis, chaos, or tragedy. In a life well lived, a man is as concerned with the growth and evolution of the people around him as he is with his own accomplishments and achievements. The idea of being present in the now rather than lost in the task is well understood. Ultimately, this translates into someone who brings those around him to discover themselves, to desire to excel, and to look inside themselves for something more refined, more complete, and more free.

But as beautiful a picture as this paints, how is it possible to consciously pursue this course? When do you know you've entered the space of your purpose, that function and role for which you were designed? Lofty questions, indeed.

All real change begins with an honest assessment of your current state and the humility to realize the deficiencies, even the atrocities, that are thriving inside. The title of this book, *Father Deficit*, implies that we were cheated out of something or deprived of the instruction and mentoring we were entitled to. As we are imperfect, it is not our fault. But neither is it anyone else's. Our deficiencies are a product of the fall of Adam and a universal truth of all of humankind.

It is true that our deficits are not our fault. But regardless of who raised us, our deficits are personal, and our deficiencies are completely our own responsibility. Who else would they belong to? The beginning of real and durable change comes from an honest understanding of who we are and the courage to admit there is a problem. And for certain, there is a problem. Unless you identify yourself as Jesus, there is a problem.

Some of the hardest things for a man to do are ask for help, seek guidance, or look for instruction. Many of us would prefer to figure things out in the privacy of our own minds. We would rather look in the mirror for the answers to our dilemmas without exposing our little souls. The problem with a mirror is that it only reflects an image, and we are very good at presenting images without content or depth. It takes a willingness to open our wounds to another man and invite him to identify the filth and contamination and lies that we carry before we can begin the surgery needed to heal.

It has been written by many authors in different ways: man was created in the image of God. We are struck by sin and rebellion, and therefore distanced and separated from God and from our true identities by forces of shame, guilt, and doubt. It is the deepest longing, the most desperate need of every man to be known, to be accepted, to be validated, to be made worthy, and to be encouraged. Therein lies the father deficit. Every man craves a father. Every man needs the impact of the Father, every day.

CHAPTER 15

Hidden Influences

EMOTIONALLY DISENGAGED, INDEPENDENT PEOPLE ALLOW THOSE closest to them to believe they can't be reached, that they don't matter, and in fact that they are not worth much to them.

A dad's relational ambivalence leads to a family who turns toward sacrificing for others to find a sense of value. Sons who desire to be heroes will be attracted to needy women and will eventually be exhausted by the demands they cannot deliver. Daughters will seek out men who need mothering but will resent the distance and immaturity these men demonstrate. They will eventually be worn out from the stress they cause. With a potential impact like those described, it would seem all men would stop and evaluate their commitment to the myth of independence. Unfortunately, the generational pattern has been deeply ingrained in masculine history. The hidden commitment to the myth of independence, generation after generation, has left men unaware of the hidden forces that shape their lives and the lives they influence.

Why have we gravitated toward the myth of masculine independence?

Fundamental to understanding the why behind most people's relational style is a willingness to embrace generational patterns. The story of independence, to be set uniquely apart, is irrefutable. It exists in every culture and is visible in many primary relationships. The will to be emotionally above or beyond the present marks people living out their independence. The independent person seeks to know without the vulnerability relationships require. The internal conflict in independent people is directly related to their unwillingness to be seen as weak. In particular, independent people are sensitive to potential rejection. They may not be consciously aware of feelings of incompetence, insecurity, and neediness that immobilize their core.

Relationships require interdependence. At the root of interdependence is an attitude fueled by a deep desire for vulnerability. Unfortunately, vulnerability, which is the ability to admit that others are needed to expand and enrich life, is seen as threatening. The threat is tied to the potential loss of autonomy. The thoughts behind refusing vulnerability are linked to a feeling of being controlled.

At some point, independent people will come to the end of their isolation. They will be required to take the single most important step in a process of release: to trust someone in areas beyond their control. They will be internally humbled but externally freed to trust. That understanding of trust can blossom into a lifestyle of relational commitment, completed by the full expression of their emotions.

The Cost of People Embracing the Myth of Independence

Independent people pay a huge price by allowing life to march on without experiencing deep, enriching relationships. Their spouses live with their partner's heart at arm's length. Their wives often say, "The man he was when we dated has disappeared." Women see the potential to love and be loved in these men, but year after year, the lack of vulnerability leaves the men closed off and disillusioned.

An independent man's emotional abandonment leaves his wife open to being preyed upon by other independent men.

That's right: an independent man on the hunt knows how to bait a vulnerable woman but chooses not to go beyond physical vulnerability in the resulting relationship. The cruelty of sensing a need in another and using it for his own gratification is lost on the independent man. His emotionally closed state allows his destructive behavior to be pushed off on the needy woman.

An independent woman longs for emotional closeness but is uncertain how to respond when approached emotionally. For many such women, life is lived without deep personal interaction. For some women, engaging in female friendship provides a safe environment to be accepted and loved. For others, there is a hope that the next guy will open the door to her heart, so rotating partners becomes a way of life.

When it comes to children, the independent person requires outward submission without a willingness to enter into open dialogue on the issues in question. Independent people may not state these rules, but the rules are felt by every child. Children learn early on how to read the silent disapproval of the people they desire to be affirmed by. The pain inside the maturing children haunts them all their lives, unless there is a point of resolution.

How Can You Disrupt the Myth of Independence?

Independent people have the unique ability to place the burden for relational health on others. It is important for independent people to stop placing emotional responsibility on others. They may love others, but in a restricted, childish, self-protective way. Independent people can move effectively toward others after admitting their fear and speaking directly to their inadequacies.

This needs to be an ongoing conversation. The tendency is for independent people to venture into an authentic dialogue and then retreat to a safe distance, feeling as though they've betrayed themselves. In fact, they've betrayed the false self they used to defend their tender hearts. In order for independent people to break free, they need to be governed by where they want to go, not by what is internally hampering them.

CHAPTER 16

Mentored to Mentoring

THERE IS A COUNTERCULTURE THAT HAS influenced the understanding of who and what a man is. There are so many definitions of what a real man looks like, the misperceptions run rampant. Before men can understand a mentoring relationship, they must understand who they are and what they want to be.

There is a misconception of masculinity often manifested in the church. This misconception undermines the biblical truth about manhood. What we can all agree on, however, is that a Christian man is to be like Jesus. If we as men are to be Christlike, then we must understand Jesus's characteristics and how Christ represented that manhood.

Jesus Christ has been described as wise, obedient, loving, kind, patient, charitable, faithful, virtuous, humble, meek, nonjudgmental, forgiving, generous, and many other positive characteristics we can envision. These are all true. But if this is what we are supposed to use as an example of manhood, then Christian men do not understand the Christ in his fullness.

Let's look at some of the other attributes of Jesus if we really want to become Christlike. These attributes must always be administered with wisdom and love. Nonetheless, they are who Christ is and what he expects from us. A note of importance is that these attributes were not a reaction but strategically applied.

Confrontational: There were many areas in which Jesus confronted others. He rebuked his disciples for their lack of faith

(Matthew 8:26). He reprimanded his generation and the religious leaders: "How long shall I put up with you?" (Mark 9:19).

Used Physical Force: Jesus used force to emphasize the moral bankrupcy of the money changers as he drove them out of the temple by turning over tables and benches (Matthew 21:12).

Used Strong Language: Jesus called the Pharisees and teachers of the law "hypocrites" (Matthew 23:13–29). He called the Pharisees "snakes" and "brood of vipers" (Matthew 23:33). He called Gentiles "dogs" (Mark 7:27). False prophets were called "wolves" (Matthew 7:17); and the generation seeking signs were called "evil," "wicked," and "perverted" (Matthew 12, 16, and 17). Jesus lived in the wilderness; he was a fisherman, hunter, and carpenter. He knew about sports, music, soldiering, and temptation. He was a man just like us (Hebrews 2:17–18, 4:15).

Being Christlike is necessary for mentorship. Knowing that Jesus used all of these attributes when mentoring his disciples and others gives a real picture of what a mentoring relationship should look like. The key to all relationships is love, honesty, compassion, and directness. These manifest themselves is all the ways Jesus dealt (and deals) with people.

Imagine if Jesus was walking the earth today, and someone brought a sinner to him to be judged, and he responded the same way he did with the woman caught in adultery: "When Jesus had raised Himself up and saw no one but the woman, He said to her, 'Woman, where are those accusers of yours? Has no one condemned you?' She said, 'No one, Lord.' And Jesus said to her, 'Neither do I condemn you; go and sin no more'" (John 8:10–11).

I can just hear the bystanders say, "What a jerk Jesus is. First he didn't condemn her, and then he went and told her how to live her life." The necessity of directness and honesty shows compassion and love. However, we fail to see compassion and love when our feelings get hurt.

A key to being mentored and mentoring is allowing truth to be spoken into your life or to speak truth into someone else's life. Sometimes truth hurts, but failure to speak truth shows the ultimate selfishness. Those who choose not to share the truth with those they are mentoring demonstrate the need to be liked more than the responsibility to care for and love someone else by sharing the truth. Jesus had no condemnation for this woman, but he cared enough to share the truth with her. Her adultery could have led her to eternal damnation. When in a mentoring situation, we need our mentors to share with us the pitfalls and minefields they see, which can derail us or plummet us into failure or sin.

Mentoring should always be direct. I know that directness has gone out of style. I can already hear the words you might say: "Who made you judge?" As with truth, directness is sometimes essential to a mentoring relationship.

As an army officer, I learned that you do not choose those you mentor; they choose you. When service members asked me to be their mentor, I let them know up front that if we were going to have a true mentoring relationship, I would be direct and give it to them in the language needed at the time. I told them I would always start with compassion, but that directness could come out firm.

A situation came up with one of the soldiers I was mentoring. After I shared with him, he aggressively and repeatedly pushed back, fully denying the situation. I looked at him and said, "Cut the bullcrap."

He looked at me in shock and responded that he appreciated our mentoring relationship, but he didn't think we could ever be friends.

The goal in a mentoring relationship is not to develop a friendship. However, I have found that in many cases, this happens after a while. In this situation, the young man needed someone to call him out. Years later, we are friends, but I doubt that would have happened if I had let him slide as his mentor.

As Jesus called out the Pharisees, the lawmakers, the Jews, and even his disciples, mentors must be willing to be direct with those they are mentoring.

Mentoring should always incorporate life experience. It amazes me to hear of people seeking counsel from others who have little or no experience. Can you imagine a newly married couple seeking advice on conflict resolution from someone who's never worked through those issues? Or from another newlywed couple that is struggling with the same issue? Proverbs 14:6–7 comes to mind: "A scoffer seeks wisdom and does not find it, But knowledge is easy to him who understands. Go from the presence of a foolish man, when you do not perceive in him the lips of knowledge."

Mentors do not have all the answers, but they will acknowledge that and help find the solution. They will always seek out advice and usually counsel with their mentor. Mentors should always have a mentor themselves, or else they won't have the experience to mentor others. I've also found unique situations in my life where I sought temporary mentoring from subject matter experts whom I didn't necessarily like. You don't have to like someone to learn something of value from them.

The mentoring relationship should have no material value attached to it. Counseling and mentoring are two different areas of influence. If you need counseling, the counselor should be professionally trained. They can help you work through issues and wounds that have become debilitating. This usually involves payment.

Mentoring is limited to a relationship based on experience and success that can be passed down through generations. Credibility is created through real experiences dealing with jobs, family, maturity, faith, and relationship. Mentoring is appropriate in circumstances where one might need wisdom to improve, but is not necessarily applicable in situations that have become debilitating. As a mentor, know when to refer a person for professional help.

When do you move from mentored to mentoring? As mentioned above, when you have life experience in an area someone needs mentoring in. Each of us will need mentoring in our lives at various times. I have had mentors and continue to have them in my life, as well as those I mentor. Both Joe and Steve have great life experiences that I just don't have. I have some that they don't have. As a mentor, I know when I can be of value and when I need to pass the ball to someone else.

To be mentored, you have to be willing to open yourself up to someone else, to allow them to speak truth into your life, and to be direct with you when needed. The relationship between Paul and Timothy is a good example:

> Let no one despise your youth, but be an example to the believers in word, in conduct, in love, in spirit, in faith, in purity. Till I come, give attention to reading, to exhortation, to doctrine. Do not neglect the gift that is in you, which was given to you by prophecy with the laying on of the hands of the eldership. Meditate on these things; give yourself entirely to them, that your progress may be evident to all. Take heed to yourself and to the doctrine. Continue in them, for in doing this you will save both yourself and those who hear you. (1 Timothy 4:12–16).

As a mentor, your words and counsel need to be guided by insight and tactfulness, or you will feel abused and misunderstood, and become angry. To be a mentor, you need to understand yourself and your limitations. Your compassion and love have to overcome your desire to be liked. If you have worked through your father deficit and continue to do so, then you are ready to help others. But remember, the best mentors will always have a mentor themselves.

CHAPTER 17

Legendary or Legacy Maker

WE HAVE A FRIEND NAMED MARCUS who is notably pure-hearted and consistent in behavior. Through development of a nonprofit organization that delivers humanitarian aid, education, and leadership, he's working toward a global impact on humanity. He has been a follower of Christ since his youth but was thrust into a tremendous sense of purpose on the heels of a near-fatal accident that temporarily took away his physical mobility. He recovered with some minor but permanent functional limitations, and his life since has been marked by a near singularity in direction. From a very humble collection of resources, Marcus set the vision and strategy for developing an independent, nonprofit ministry that is impacting nations of people today. His plan began with a calling and a sympathetic heart toward a need, with a strategy characterized by an unswaying commitment to its purpose.

Early in the process, Marcus sought counsel from several more experienced and older individuals from different facets of the faith-based and secular world. From those connections, an advisory board was created with members who believed in his vision and desired to help it come to fruition. Marcus asked this board for assistance in design and decision-making that would provide growth and development as well as overcome barriers to progress. Specifically, he intentionally gave this panel of advisors encouragement to keep him focused on his purpose, by holding him accountable to the vision and redirecting the strategy when it failed to serve the goals. In other words, he actively sought counsel from others who demonstrated effective character in their own lives and were committed to acting out of love and courage to help him grow.

The culmination of Marcus's journey has yet to be determined, as he is still very young and has years to continue toward his goals. However, he is exemplary in several respects. First, he lives under a firm commitment to his belief system, centered on his faith in Christ (what he stands for). Second, he has taken ample time to formulate a plan and define a long-term direction for his life (a defined purpose). Finally, he makes important decisions and choices daily in a consistent manner, ensuring they are compatible with his beliefs and supportive of his life purpose.

Knowing he cannot exist and succeed solely out of his own volition and ability, Marcus intentionally invited others with similar principles and positive character traits to augment those areas in which he is weak. He has adopted a disposition and posture that invites purposeful advice and critically evaluates what he learns from others, so that he may improve and become more effective.

As a result of his organized way of thinking, and thus behaving, Marcus has designed a life model for success by utilizing a directed and focused method of decision-making and inviting the strengths of others to fully realize what is possible in his own life. He is creating a legacy that will reach far beyond his immediate life on this earth.

——

Eric grew up around a drinking culture in which alcohol was a focal point of many social interactions. He was gregarious, fun to be around, and indulgent. He married, became a father of two children, and obtained a good job in the trade industry.

Eric hid his habit from his wife and told lies to cover his

path. His marriage and parenting suffered, and he made the decision to quit drinking and join Alcoholics Anonymous (AA). His faith became a guiding factor in his life. He intentionally became involved with other men who offered both humility and grace, and his path got back on track.

Eric and his wife developed a passion for engaging with people who were suffering from infidelity, addiction, loss, divorce, or struggles around parenting. He is not forward or in any respect aggressive in his approach toward helping others. Eric is effective simply because he is willing to walk alongside those who are suffering, without judgment, possessing a humble spirit and a caring heart.

He is not overly passionate about his job, but he has stayed committed and is very good at what he does. He is an exemplary employee because of the man he has become. He has been patient and methodical in his course, not expecting sudden miracles, but plodding along day by day and growing in the process. He continues to attend AA meetings, some three decades later, and continues to be involved with like-minded men who speak to him honestly and offer him humility and grace. He does not waver from the intentional practices that have kept him in alignment with his vision.

Eric has been an amazing husband and father. His children have married and become parents, and he is now a grandfather, passing along an entirely new level of mentorship and guidance to another generation. He is leaving a tremendous legacy.

———

There is no purpose in comparing the magnitude of legacies left by individuals. The value of one life is not comparable to the value of another. The only truth in the question is that they both have value, and both lives matter. However, in each circumstance, choices have been made and intentions have been directed in the interests of making a difference, of generating a positive impact. That is very impressive indeed.

And then there are legends. Notoriously good or notoriously

bad, legends are about the individual. Whether one seeks a name that can strike fear into a nation of people, or to be known as the only person who can belch the entire national anthem, a legend depicts personal accomplishment or infamy that does not necessarily leave a lasting impact.

In this context, eliminating the father deficit is about creating a legacy and not a legend. It is about seeking to become fully developed and fully mature. It is about fully realizing the purpose for which you were originally created.

So where can we go from here? What personal steps are needed to fill the father deficit? This book has described the tools, resources, and techniques to apply in order to sustain a solid foundation for the future.

First, allow clarity to inform your choices. It is a requirement that you reevaluate how well you know yourself and have a willingness to discard the persona you have projected regarding who you think you ought to become. You have to take the time, make the effort, and endure the discomfort needed to discover who you *really* are at the core and honestly unravel the influences that have derailed your progress and led you off target. This includes a willingness to embrace your inability to love yourself without having someone else constantly demonstrate your worth.

Your perception of your personal sin is that it's an order of magnitude greater than the sin of others. Because it is your own, the ways you have disappointed, hurt, or cheated others are loud, palpable, and gut-wrenching. But if it were any other way, you would not have a conscience.

The chiseling away of your pride, stubbornness, and independence is necessary to come to terms with your identity. You were created out of love and made unique, with your own personality, your own giftedness, your own value, and your own specific purpose. It is your job to determine what that entails.

Accomplishing this requires an acceptance of the fact that each of us has been designed and brought to life by the loving Creator of the universe. No personality elsewhere has demonstrated love for you more directly than Jesus Christ. Your worth was worth his dying to redeem you. Until you have clarity on this point, your personal worth will be confounded by a lopsided view of who you are; you cannot appreciate that you truly matter.

Luke 21:27–28 says, "At that time they will see the Son of Man coming in a cloud with power and great glory. When these things begin to take place, stand up and lift up your heads, because your redemption is drawing near."

Once you discover who you are, it becomes important to clarify where you are going. To step beyond where you are to where you want to be requires courage. The unknown and unexperienced can be a daunting place to desire and apprehend. The lack of control can cause you to pull back, opt for the status quo, and refuse to adopt the positive reinforcement coming from others.

Courage is required for you to fully love yourself, honestly love others, and risk yourself for more: more meaning, more influence, and more positive impact, the ongoing process of restructuring your internal world. Eventually, the process of self-discovery will lead to a well-defined vision of durable purpose for your life going forward, providing a focal point and directing you to live on target.

Along the way, it will be critical to align your core values to the system of beliefs you have chosen to follow. Alignment happens when all choices and decisions occur in direct relationship to your beliefs and your realized purpose. Working together, alignment of self, beliefs, and purpose will lead to fewer wasted moments, fewer bad decisions, and far less regret and disappointment. When you live in alignment, the right behaviors and the right choices become easy and ultimately second nature (intuitive).

In an atom, two electrons cannot occupy the same energy space at the same time. So they spin in opposite directions, and their resulting magnetic forces cancel each other out. However, some compounds contain unpaired electrons whose spin can produce a directional magnetic force. When a majority of unpaired electrons are spinning in the same direction, a macroscopic magnetic force is produced that is strong enough to feel. Alignment of energy in a common direction becomes a powerful force.

The developmental process will be enhanced if you create a safe environment for others to give you honest feedback. You cannot identify all of the opportunities for improvement without assistance from others who desire to help you grow. Giving permission for others to speak honestly into your life invites encouragement and necessary critical thinking to effectively identify areas you are weak in.

No person is an expert in all areas, and even fewer admit to needing help. The sad fact is, everyone could become stronger and more productive by using the power and energy that others are willing to offer. Few of us can reach beyond our own insecurity to fully realize the strength that others can provide. Listening to learn rather than to defend will accelerate the process.

Engage a trusted, proven friend who has proven loyal to your well-being. All men need an effective mentor. Mentors are effective not because of their talents but because of their willingness to uncover their hearts and risk personal vulnerability to the benefit of others. Trust between men is essential for this step to be realized.

Strategically wait, allowing time to create an honest momentum. Focus on impact rather than outcomes. Weigh positivity by how it opens your heart to others and how their hearts respond. Strategic waiting can create anticipation, longing, and hope. Stay engaged philosophically when a waiting period is operational. Infect others with your commitment to the process of change.

The wisdom of Solomon will continue to prevail well beyond our transient presence in this world: "There is nothing new under the sun" (Ecclesiastes 1:9). Every discovery has been recounted in history, every idea has been previously espoused in one form or another, and every tragedy has its equal. Let's not lose sight of the fact that our accomplishments will never compare to the magnitude of the relationships we have with those around us. Ultimately, your legacy will not be reflected by the episodes of success and the legendary feats you've recorded, but by the way you touched the hearts of those near you in your journey. The true legacy will be a reflection of how you lived, as opposed to the structures you built in the process.

Clarity. Courage. Engage. Wait.

The tale of a man is depicted in those around him. Creating a long-term vision, an actual target that your choices, your plans, and your development will lead you to, is a powerful way to begin the journey. Take the time to look beyond the troubles and distractions of today. Visualize what you desire for your life and how it will be recorded. Set your path in the direction of that target, and begin. What will be your legacy?

CPSIA information can be obtained
at www.ICGtesting.com
Printed in the USA
LVHW04s1923010618
579312LV00001B/2/P